THE PROCESS

The Process

There is a process for everything to move forward faster

FRANCIS ZIPETO

Ingram Spark

CONTENTS

Dedicated to Cidalia:
Without her, none of this story could be told.
I love you to the moon and back

Special Thank you to
my daughter Lorelei. She inspires me daily.

INTRODUCTION: HOW THIS BOOK CAME TO BE WRITTEN

I have spent most of my adult life searching for what drives people to get what they want or decide to settle for less than they can be. If you speak to many Americans or people in the western world, you will find out that the *"American Dream"* is still possible.

What is the *"American Dream"* anyway? Who sets the rules of what it is? More importantly, how do we know we have arrived? These are questions I have asked myself time and time again.

I grew up in Brockton, Massachusetts, with people who lived on both sides of the tracks. For the first twelve years of my life, I lived on the Southside, and after that, until I was twenty-three, on the Eastside. At the time, I didn't see much difference from one side to the other, looking back on it now I see the huge differences.

The Southside is where all the projects were, and crime was considerably higher. I recall one of the major reasons we moved was because someone was chased through our front yard by the police carrying a gun while my sisters and I were outside playing.

As I remember it, after moving to the Eastside, I didn't see much of a police presence at all. We called that area of town *"The forgotten side"* of the city. Home values were higher, stores were cleaner, average income was higher, and we noticed that people who lived in our new neighborhood had lived there for decades.

When I think about the *"American Dream"* as an adult, it is obvious. There were processes people followed on both sides of the tracks. Both achieved a different result, and regardless of the differences in the result, there was a process.

Many people on the Southside believed they were born into a lifestyle, and that was all they were worthy of achieving. They were defined by a certain income, and crime was a common occupation, which they believed was their destiny. They followed the process of their immediate environment, which shaped who they became.

The Eastside was not satisfied with the status quo. Their parents and families demanded more of them than they had for themselves. People believed there was more out there and were determined to get it. They also followed the process of their immediate environment, and it shaped who they became.

What drives this home for me is that I am still very close with most of my neighborhood friends from the Eastside. We still get together around Christmas time to catch up and reflect on old times. One of my best friends from that time in my life is someone I still see monthly.

Every December my wife and I do what we call *"Disappearing December,"* where we leave our home in Orlando, Florida, and travel back to our original home towns in Massachusetts, to spend the month with our family. Last December I was driving through the Southside of Brockton when I heard a voice yell my name. I pulled over and there was the kid next door to where I lived on the Southside. He was panhandling and said he just wasn't doing well. He had just gotten out of rehab and was struggling and living in a homeless shelter.

I remember that both of his parents had trouble with drugs, and it looks like for him, he was not able to change the family pattern. Here I am standing in front of what I felt was a mirror of what could have been my destiny had my parents not made the decision they did. I wished him well, and for days after, that interaction haunted me.

It again made me think about the *"American Dream."* This kid, now a man, was not only not living the *"American Dream,"* he was living a nightmare, that he can not wake up from, or that has any end in sight. Is it too late for this man to achieve the *"American Dream?"* Will he ever have a stable career, family, or a home of his own? I believe it's never too late. My intention for my reader is to understand that for everything you want, there is a how.

There is not a single thing in this life that anyone wants in which someone hasn't already blazed the trail for us to follow. We must be resourceful enough to go out and find it. There is a saying that we will talk about in a future chapter that says, *"We don't know what we don't know."* I am a firm believer that everyone is doing the best they can with what they know and have experienced. I do not believe anybody is born bad or born with an instinct to harm anyone. Those are all learned behavior and beliefs.

We are all amateurs, including our parents. When we had children or our parents had us, there was no handbook. We lead others by using whatever knowledge and past experiences we have access to at that moment in time. The more we know and the more we grow, following the right process will not only change the course of our destiny but also the destinies of everyone we interact with.

This story I shared about living on both sides of the tracks is what inspired me to write this book. I knew I couldn't be the only one who wanted more or knew someone who was in a downward spiral who wanted out and did not have the how.

There will always be people who rise against all odds, as there will always be people who settle for less than their potential. There is a great quote from the movie *"A Bronx Tale."* *"There is nothing worse than wasted talent."* My mission in writing this book is that I open your eyes to the opportunities you have and that you discover your fullest potential and get exactly what you want in your life.

~ I ~

WHAT'S A PROCESS?

"Without continual growth and progress, such words as improvement, achievement, and success have no meaning. "- Benjamin Franklin

As a business coach of some of the most diverse and forward-thinking companies, and the owner of multiple businesses myself, I am often asked what is the key to success. Unlike the key to your car or home, there are several keys to success. One door opens up the next until you are exactly where you want to be.

Before you can access the keys, however, you need a foundation, on which to build the frame. That foundation is how the right processes are built. There is a sequence of events that have to happen for success in anything to take place. Every time a structure is built whether it be big or small, it has to rise from the bottom up. The process of building would never start with the roof first. That would be a disaster.

Could you imagine building a 100 story building, and within a few weeks of completing it, the building tips over? You find out after your investigation that the reason it tipped over was that someone forgot to add the rebar when the concrete was poured. You don't need an engineering degree to know that without the rebar inside the concrete, it has no strength and will crumble under any weight. People miss-steps, not just in construction, but in all areas of their lives.

Not following a process to move forward on projects, business plans, personal finance, key relationships, and just about anything else, will prove to be an uphill and insurmountable journey. One of the greatest things about living now is that for the most part, everything we would like to achieve has already been modeled in a process one way or another.

A process is nothing more than a proven system, or path, that one can follow that has demonstrated to get the results you are looking for. We can name anything on Earth we want, in our personal and professional lives, and somewhere there is a system for it. Have you heard the phrase, *"Don't reinvent the wheel?"*

I remember just out of high school going straight into the workforce as a remodeling carpenter in south shore Massachusetts. We were a very small crew, just the owner, lead carpenter, and myself as an apprentice. It was like working with Star Wars characters, Yoda and Obi-Wan Kenobi, and I was a young Luke Skywalker. These guys had a process for everything we did.

We specialized in remodeling kitchens and bathrooms. This was 1999 when solid surface countertop kitchens were just getting popular and everyone wanted a multi-jet shower. No matter the address of the home or the town it was in when a new job was started it was the same process every time. We would go in to rip out and demo the old, do any necessary reframing, send in the plumbers and electricians, close walls and floors back up with new material, and bring in the new cabinets, counters, or shower and vanity.

Being able to predict how long each stage of the process would take allowed the owner to know exactly how many projects we could do in a year and how far out we could book work. This way he knew how many more projects he had to find so we were never out of work.

Did this process work flawlessly every time? Of course not. There was something on every project that we did not expect. When this happened the team had a process for being able to pivot and solve the problem. Success lies in asking, " *What did we do the last time this happened?*"

Sometimes things would happen we had never experienced before. For our team, we knew a man who was the craftsman of all craftsmen, and he lived in the same town we were based out of. His name was Walley. Walley was the building inspector and had a lifetime of experience with just about everything that could go wrong in construction.

When the three of us were scratching our heads looking for an answer, we would call upon Walley's experience and mentorship to get us through and win the day. Once we got the knowledge we needed it went into our process moving forward. Having the answer for yourself is not always necessary. Getting outside mentorship is part of the success process.

People like Walley are all around us if we look in the right places. I have had the privilege of having many Walley's in my life. All of them have their fingerprints all over any success I have achieved. They are people who enter our lives for different periods. You may have a Walley that you get to spend years or even decades with. Other times a Walley may just be in your life a matter of days, weeks, or months.

I anticipate having many more people like Wally come into my life as I live and grow. Let's take writing this book for example. I did not have the foggiest idea of how to get a book published and into the hands of people who would want to read it. Come to think of it, I didn't even know how to write the book! What needs to be in it? How long should it be? What order do I put the chapters in? I had so many questions.

Thankfully I was blessed to have someone in my life who has written a couple of books and could guide me through this process. Constantly helping every step of the way with his wisdom. If not for him, you may have never had the opportunity to read this. It may still be a pile of thoughts written on my laptop.

People you will meet

You will read inspirational interviews explaining how three very young entrepreneurs are achieving massive results by following a process. All three believe in success through others and are resourceful enough to navigate the tough times and find a process that works.

A perfect example of someone who went out and found a Walley to go further faster is Chris Nikic. Chris Nikic was the first person with Down syndrome to ever complete an IronMan race. My interview with him is in the last section of this book. In the interview, you will hear him talk about how he scoured the area looking for someone to help him bridge the gap of his dream for inclusion, and make it a reality.

The person Chris found was Dan Grieb. The bond formed between these two men is amazing. The obstacles they had to overcome to get Chris to a level where he could even enter an IronMan race, are nothing short of spectacular, never mind completing the race.

In the interview with Chris, many processes will be shared that were uncovered and are ongoing. He reveals that the IronMan race was just the first step in a very long series of milestones that have very little to do with being an elite athlete. One of the most inspiring processes Chris and Dan created is they share is the process of being 1% better.

There is an interview with a man who is on course to accomplish everything he could have ever dreamed up by the age of 30. David Berlant is a businessman from Central Florida who is relentless in his pursuit of excellence. I had the privilege of working side by side with David for a few years in the real estate industry let me say the inspiration you will get from reading his story is beyond words.

David has discovered vehicles that fund the life he has always wanted. He too found the right person to partner with to move him from point A to point B in a fraction of the time he would have on his own. Most notable was what led him to meet his bride-to-be.

Our third interview is with a chef who just wanted more than to be a cook. He wanted to use his skills and talents to change the entire food experience. Tyler Trainer tells a story of many processes, starting from when he was a young boy. Using inspiration and encouragement from his family to start down his path, Tyler is changing the way people prepare for holidays and do their weekly meal preparation.

One of the most amazing parts of the whole story is that he decided to start this business in the middle of the Covid-19 pandemic in 2020. While most of the world was barricading themselves in their homes, and the food industry as a whole was being crushed,

Tyler said " I think it's my time to serve the community." You will find many processes you can translate to your life and work in this interview.

There is one thing you will notice about all three of the incredible people I interviewed. They are all still in the middle of their process. No one has said, *"I did it and now I am done."* This was by design for two reasons. Number one, I don't believe we are ever really done with processes until we are dead. Number two, this book was intended to help people take action and inspire them to take their lives to the next level no matter their background.

There are plenty of books you can read with stories and interviews from people who are known celebrities or experts who can show you how they did something once they believe they are finished doing it. What I wanted to show was people finding success and getting results while striving for more. That is what is real.

These are real people and real stories of everyday people just like us. It shows that to find someone who can help you find and follow the right process, you may not have to leave your zip code. Then again you might, and if you do, are you willing to get in a car, or train, or plane, to find the answers you need? My idea since you are reading this book is you are willing. Not only willing, but equipped with the tools to find the processes that are right for you and your future. Let's get to it.

Stop before you hurt yourself

The world is filled with people who have great visions and ideas and don't know where to start. Some take it upon themselves to say, *"Let me just get started and go with what I know, and I can make it up as I go along."* They figure they have enough natural talent to be able to at least get started, and will learn as they go. After all, look how far they have come over the years with only their natural talents.

NO!!! STOP!!! This is how you hurt yourself. As coaches, we call this the entrepreneurial approach. This is a fancy way of saying it's the amateur way. I have had clients on the brink of losing everything because they relied on their natural talent to take them as far as they could go on their own, and have no plan for what to do next.

I remember working with a real estate investor not too long ago who came to me for help in growing sales volume and profits. It was a small company, just the investor and one administrative assistant. On the very first call, I asked to see his profit and loss statement and transaction history for the past twelve months.

He did not have either to share. He could only speak in approximations because the company had tracked nothing. They went on the assumption they were profitable based on whether or not there was money in the bank account at the end of the month. When I asked, *"How many homes did the company have to view to be able to buy one?"* he was at a loss for words and again could only approximate. This made it impossible for the company to know if it was winning.

The company had been in business for a decade and when we looked back over the financials they had made a decent profit. We discovered that the company was producing well below its potential. Over the next few weeks and months, we put some processes in place from other successful companies in this field. Within three months the company had a track record of successes it had never had before.

Every year prior, the success of the company was solely dependent on the owner's ability to go out with his natural talents and make it happen. This was not a sustainable model. The owner of the business said he worked far fewer hours and achieved a higher level of success by following the processes that we had found and implemented.

The process of knowing how many houses he needed to view to find one he wanted to buy was what made the entire cycle work. Before he would just wake up, hit the ground, and go. No direction, no plan, no calendar. Just go. When he knew his numbers and could schedule the number of property viewings he needed in a day to find success, the rest of his day fell into place. He was far more productive.

The same goes for his financial statements. Once he knew how many homes they needed to view to hit the financial goals of the company, all he had to do was schedule enough viewings to get the contracts he needed to hit the profit goal. His exact words were, " *I finally feel like a business person.*" That is the power of a process.

There is a backstory for this business owner. He worked in a real estate investment firm before he opened his own. He worked as a property acquisitions manager. So he was in charge of going to find the properties for the firm to buy and then getting them under contract. A very straightforward role.

One day he decided that he didn't want to work for someone else. He wanted to do this on his own. Seems simple enough right?

He would create a business entity name, open a bank account, build a client base, send out marketing, and boom he finds success. Until he almost didn't. He almost drove himself into bankruptcy. He had the process down for going to find a property and putting it under contract, but what about the other pieces of the business? What about marketing, bookkeeping, customer service, and transaction paperwork. He had never been involved in that side of the business.

He had no idea how many pieces of marketing he needed to mail to get a lead. We had to find a process for that. He had no idea how to manage his finances. We found a process for that. He needed to keep the clients happy and the paperwork in compliance. The time it took to find the answers and processes to turn this business into a company was just a few months. He had been operating in chaos for years. He lost a relationship over never being home, and can only see his son now on the weekends. What are you willing to lose by not using systems and processes?

He said to me as he started to get control of the company and the life he was striving for, " *If I operated this way from the beginning, I never would have lost my marriage and have to wait for the weekend to see my son.*" There were tears in his eyes and he said, " *This has been a humbling experience.*" That is how you can be hurt by following the process.

The American Dream

In recent years many have asked the question... Is the American Dream still possible? You would be blown away at some of the responses I get when I ask this question. Things like, " *That's Gramma's world.*" or, " *What millennium are you in?*". There is an enormous number of people who live in this country who do not believe it is possible and don't even strive for it.

On the other hand, some people have been fleeing their homelands for centuries to come here for one thing and one thing only. *"The American Dream."* They come to a place where possibilities are endless, where one day you work in a factory and the next you can open your own business if you work hard.

The American Dream itself is a process, a process that has been established over a hundred and fifty years before this country was a country. It's about being able to have a place where people could come and be free to make their own choices and live the lives they choose. It is a process from start to finish.

Even before the founding fathers, we had the Pilgrims. The Pilgrims set the precedent for hundreds of years of future immigrants to make a life on American soil. Since the early 1600s, the land of the free was a place where you could escape from the life you were born into and start fresh. All you had to do was get here and there were opportunities everywhere for those who chose to take them.

Four hundred years later, the process is the same. We have people by the thousands who look at the United States as a place to build their lives. Living in Orlando, Florida, we are a melting pot of just about everyone from every country here, all striving to be the best versions of themselves.

In the same breath, we are looking at a time in history when the American Dream is being challenged. Millions of Americans had the privilege to be born here who think the pathway to the American Dream does not involve hard. Somewhere in the last twenty to twenty-five years, the fire to go into the world and make it their own has diminished.

To achieve the American Dream, when people came here as immigrants or started a new job as American citizens, they started from the bottom and worked their way up. No one started as the CEO and automatically got a six-figure income. There was time that had to be put in to learn your craft and work up the ladder of success. This is a proven model from generation to generation.

However, millions don't think this process is valid in the current environment. Millions of people think they will just be given the six-figure job, just because they have a degree. Starting from the bottom and working your way to the top seems to be becoming a thing of the past. Not because this generation isn't smart, because they have proven to be brilliant. There is just a sense of the, "*give it to me now attitude*", that prevents them from moving forward faster. There is an entire generation of people who are retiring and fewer people to take their places.

My wife and I recently took a trip across the country in our RV. We traveled through twelve states from the east coast to the west coast. In every state we traveled through, we came across labor shortage signs, places that had to close early and open late, and some places that had to close for entire days for a labor shortage.

How can this be? How is it that you have some people who are just working their fingers to the bone, and others who would rather stay home and not work? Some people will blame it on the government for making it too easy for people to get assistance or unemployment benefits. That is easy to do rather than looking deeper and asking the question of why? What possesses a person to pass up opportunities to have a career and pursue their dreams and instead take the short-term easy route of staying home?

I am not talking about the people who suffer from disabilities or illnesses. I am talking about the ones who work the system so they do not have to go to work. What dreams can they achieve by taking an easier short-term solution rather than taking their life by the horns?

Without a process for success, people feel lost. If there are millions of people who don't believe the American Dream is possible, how did they get that way? What environment was created for them to see what can be accomplished in a lifetime through focus and hard work? Take the average factory worker or school teacher, for example. They work tirelessly day after day, week after week, month after month, and year after year. All striving for one goal... the "American Dream." Let's define the "American Dream" just for a moment. **It is simply to build the life you desire and to do what you want when you want, and with whom you want.**

Many people ask, Is this still possible? Whether you say it is or it isn't, you are right. If you believe that living the *"American Dream"* was Grandma's world and in this Millenium, it is just not possible, then that is your reality. If you are already setting up for it, and believe you are well on your way to achieving it now and in the future, that is your reality.

There is a process to accomplish every single goal you can set for yourself. Here is the kicker. You need to seek it out and then follow it. In our Grandparents' America, they were able to achieve this dream by working long hours for very little money and keeping expenses to an absolute minimum. That was their process, and they sought it out and followed it.

A process is just an operating system that has been proven to work time and time again. The process of the *"American Dream"* is one of the longest proven systems you will find in the world. In the rest of this book, I hope you will see that through all the different systems we will talk about, you can use them to create your own American Dream.

~ II ~

HARD WORK IS STILL HARD WORK

"It's not about money or connections – it's the willing-ness to outwork and outlearn everyone."
-Mark Cuban

Having the opportunity to own multiple businesses and coaching several more, I would have to be not paying attention not to see common themes and patterns in human behavior. Whether you were born in the United States, Europe, Asia, or Africa, humans still have the basic needs to grow and connect.

If you study every generation dating back to the days of the pilgrims, you will see there is always a portion of the population who did what it took to rise to the top, and a group that floundered and could barely stay above water. Why is it that when settlers first came to the United States within weeks and months some had crops and land blossoming and others could not make it through the first winter? Or more recently, how can a country have gone through what we now call " *The Great Depression*", and some found amazing wealth and riches and some could barely put food on the table?

If you study human beings and civilizations dating back thousands of years, you will see similar patterns and trends. What was it that the first Pilgrim families did through those first couple of winters to survive, while others struggled? Resourcefulness. The Pilgrims who thrived followed a process and did not quit until they found the right one.

The ones who survived winter didn't do it without facing adversity. Failure was not an option. They just found a way to thrive and succeed. In the past four hundred years, you could argue that this generation of people may have had to be the most resourceful. They came to a place where no one had ever settled and accomplished it with very limited resources. When adversity hits us, it is not a lack of resources that stops us from succeeding. It is a lack of resourcefulness.

In every generation, we will see people who are resourceful enough to find the process for their success and follow it, and we also see the people searching for the magic pill and taking shortcuts. Hard work is still hard work! Whichever path you chose to start your journey, whether it be working a 9-5 job or starting your own business. Hard work will be one of the most important ingredients.

Starting at the bottom and working your way up takes an enormous amount of hard work. Showing up early and going home late is sometimes required, and sometimes is still not enough. Hard work will only get us so far. Being resourceful, and going to find the answers to your questions about what the next rung up the ladder of your journey is will be the secret ingredient for all your success thereafter.

So many times we hear reasons about why people don't have what they want. *"I don't have the money or the time. I am too young or too old.*" These are exactly that, *REASONS*. If you believe you are too old or don't have enough money, then you're right. If you believe you can achieve whatever you want no matter what your financial situation or age, you're right too.

Whatever the story is that you keep telling yourself is what your results will be. The story you tell yourself is like playing a song on repeat. It will just keep playing over and over. Your results will also be on repeat. If you tell yourself you can, and go find the answers, then you achieve the result you asked for. If you say you're too old or don't have the money, you'll achieve that result as well.

David Berlant, who you will meet later on in the interview portion of the book, worked side by side with me in the real estate industry for a few years. At the time, David was not even 25 years old. His primary focus was working to help people sell their homes for a top price and buy a new construction home from one of our developers. In Central Florida, at that time, new construction was what everyone wanted.

In the beginning, David struggled to get both the sellers and the builder representatives to take him seriously. He was very young and had a baby face. He owned no real estate at that time and had a hard time achieving credibility. For more than a year, he had to scrape to make things happen for him.

As you will learn in his interview, he is relentless. Achieving the results he was looking for was never a doubt in his mind. Day after day, week after week, and month after month, David would show up and commit to improving his craft. He attached himself to a couple of mentors and began the rise to the top.

David's confidence rose so fast, it could have been mistaken for cockiness. Cocky was the last thing David was. What he did discover, and fast, was that clients and other salespeople needed to see confidence to believe he was the right person to work with. The confidence made them look past how young he was.

So here is an example of someone who easily could have put their head in the sand and said, " *I am just too young.*" This process shows that "*I am too old*" or "*I am too young*", is just a belief someone put in your head that is like the song that keeps playing over and over. We will explore this more deeply in the interview.

Let's say you are fresh out of college and you have a Bachelor's degree. You are ambitious and ready to take on the world. You spent well over six figures to get your degree and you feel entitled to make a six-figure income right out of the gates. You go to company after company, some who have some of the best at what they do working there. Company after company says they are starting new employees at fifty thousand a year. What do you do?

This is an all too common story for many people fresh out of school. They want to be out on their own, and now have student loan payments bigger than a house mortgage, and can not find a starting job to make what they think they are worth. The story of what immigrant families did to achieve success should be applied here.

They came to this country with nothing and most didn't speak the language. They had to take low-paying jobs to get started and they worked their way to the top. They were resourceful enough to find people in their position who achieved results and modeled what they did.

Now back to our college student scenario. The graduate could take the position paying less than they hoped, then find the best people in the company at what they do and be mentored by them.

How quickly could they show enough value to the company to get that six-figure income? The answer is not that long at all. Maybe one or two years of mastering their craft.

This process, which has been in place for generations demonstrates hard work is still hard work. This can be said for anybody working to achieve anything. Hard work is not the only answer to success, but without it, results don't show up on their own. The formula of hard work and resourcefulness will win every time.

"I'm a great believer in luck, and I find the harder I work the more I have of it."

Thomas Jefferson

What drives you?

The answer to this single question is what separates the people who have a good life from those who have an outstanding life. The things that make our motor run like family, travel, charity, recreation, or contributing to others, are what drive us forward. What If you were in a sales position, and all day long you had to make cold calls to create a business? Day in and day out you got a lot more no's than yeses and it burned you out. You ask yourself, " *Why am I doing this?*", "*There must be an easier way.*"

The first question is the most important. Why? What motivates someone to get up every day to go to the office and strive to be the best at what they do? Some people say they just don't know what their "*why*" is. What is "*The Process*" of discovering the why? The first is motivation. Think about what it was that made you want to start down this path. This is an extremely important piece. Something moved you to get started. We need to go back and find out what that was.

We want to keep these goals to two or three things total. The reason is goals should never be a checklist. They should be very specific. You can then very clearly pursue them on a daily, weekly, and monthly basis. Pursuing too many goals at one time will overwhelm you and you will lose interest.

The second section is financial. This is anything financial you would like to achieve. This includes both personal and business. These are like paying off debt, saving a certain amount of money, or having a certain amount of cash flow. This also can be broken down to yearly, monthly, weekly, and then daily. It is important to tie our financial goals to our business or work goals to be sure the business or work goals are big enough to support the financial goal.

I remember one year my wife and I were making dream boards on New Year's Eve, as we do every year. I had many business accomplishments I wanted to achieve and a few personal ones as well. One of the personal goals I had was to purchase bicycles so we could ride on cool evenings and weekends.

At the end of that year, I reflected on what I had accomplished and almost every single goal I made for business was achieved. Had made more money that year than ever before. On the personal side, I never purchased the bicycles. The reason had nothing to do with money, it had to do with the fact that I was not paying attention to the personal goals I had set. I was focused daily and weekly only on my financial and business goals.

I did end up buying the bicycles, but it wasn't until I slowed down and stopped to look at my personal goals. Don't be the person who has all the business and financial success you ever wanted and then do nothing for yourself. The whole purpose of going down the path of a process is to have what we want in our personal life first.

The third, and most important piece of all, is personal. None of the *"Why"* circles can be complete, or worth doing, without our personal why. When we think about fulfilling our personal why it is ok to be selfish and go big. Most of us spend so much of our time worrying about others, we rarely take the time to take care of ourselves.

Personal why's could be about fitness, spending more time with your family, or vacations you would like to take. Everyone has different things that move them and get them up every day. We need to keep the things that are most precious to us and fulfill us the most at the top of our calendar.

The model I use for this is simple, not easy. I have the most energy in the morning and that is when scheduling what fulfills me most makes the most sense. For instance, I get fulfillment from playing golf with my friends. Life can get in the way, so I make sure I am as close to the first tee time in the morning as possible to get what fulfills me the most done first thing in the morning.

Checking in on your Why.

So many people start down a path and then look back a decade later and realize the things that were important to them ten years ago are no longer important. It is critical to continually check in to make sure what you say your why was is still relevant to where your life is today. Life will throw curveballs constantly and it will make us change our direction. Sometimes the change is slight and sometimes it is drastic.

Let's take one of the three sections of the *"why"* we just spoke about. You can pick any of the three you want, and if you think long enough, you will think of a time when something you didn't expect to happen changed your course. If this happens enough times, different things become important to us. I remember I was 26 years old, started a new relationship, changed construction companies I was working for, and moved to a new town. It was a scary time in my life and exciting at the same time. At 26, I was not in the goal-setting portion of my life yet, but I had a vision of how I would like things to turn out that year and years after.

Four years later I was 30 years old and this is how fast things change. I was no longer in the relationship I started at 26, I was no longer in construction full time, and was no longer living in the town I had moved to. A completely different life was in front of me, and if you told me that was going to be my life just four years earlier, I would have said *"no way."*

The things I thought were important to me at 26 were no longer were valid at age 30. I had just joined one of the biggest real estate firms in the world, I had almost all new people surrounding me on a day to day, and as a business owner, was learning and growing faster than my brain could process. I felt like each one of those four years was like dog years.

Things shift and change so fast in our lives we need to always check in on what we are moving towards to make sure it is still valid. Weekly check-ins on monthly goals and quarterly check-ins on one and five-year goals are good practices. Committing to weekly check-ins where you are in the process of the week and month keeps the goals fresh and exciting. They will also bring clarity to know if you're still working on what is most important, and you won't need to pivot. Checking in quarterly on the big stuff will have the same result.

We ask ourselves three questions while reviewing our goals.

Question 1: Am I on track?

Question2: Are these goals still important?

Question3: Do I need to pivot?

Question 1 allows us to reflect on the gap we have on any of the goals we are working towards. We call this the "*GAP TRAP.*" The gap trap can sneak up on you if you're not watching. Week one of the month you're off by a little, then week two same thing. Before you know it, you're off by a lot.

When we check in frequently, it minimizes surprises. It eliminates you getting to September of a year and asking, " *What happened? How did I get this far behind?*" If this has ever happened to you, it is simply because you took your eye off the ball, and time became your worst enemy. If you can spend 15 minutes a week just checking to be sure you are on track, you can make any minor adjustments you need to make up for anything you are behind on.

Question 2 is the gut check. Are these goals still important? The whole point of having a why, and making goals to achieve them, is to motivate you to get out of bed. If when you look at the goals in front of you and they are no longer important, then is it motivating at all? At that point, they are just a bunch of words on a sheet of paper.

I hear these words multiple times a year: "*I don't feel connected to my goals.*" That is just simply because you were at a different point in your life when these things mattered, and now you have different priorities. This happens to everyone. It happens in our work, our relationships, and with ourselves. If things always stayed the same, how boring would that be?

Question 3 is the result of the first two. Do I need to pivot? This requires a two-part answer. The first part is if you are not on track, what actions and habits do we have to pivot to so we get back on track? The only reason we got off track in the first place is that something distracted you, and that is where you decided to put your time. It is perfectly acceptable to pivot. You don't need permission. These are **YOUR** goals. If you need to pivot, by all means, pivot.

The second part of the answer comes from the answer in Question 2. If at any point you feel what you are moving towards is no longer important, then pivot and pivot fast. Every day that goes by is a day we don't get back, so we should spend it going for something that matters to us. Many people are living lives that have other people's visions attached to them. They are not living a life based on their terms. This process gives you the power to be the author of your own life story.

~ III ~

A PLAN VS. A GOAL

"Our goals can only be reached by the vehicle of a plan, in which we must fervently believe, and upon which we must vigorously act. There is no other route to success."
—Pablo Picasso

Dreams are what keep us moving forward. They give us the motivation to pursue what, at one point in our lives, seemed impossible. Children are the best at this. They dream of growing up and being a princess, or a firefighter, police officer, even President of the United States. Dreaming is what made Walt Disney a household name.

Imagine if Walt Disney hadn't dreamt about building a place where families could fulfill their dreams. He had a dream and a vision, and by taking his dream and putting it into a plan it became a reality. Does that seem like a process to you?

You bet it does! The process of building your Disney is as simple as being bold enough to dream big enough that people laugh at you when you tell them your dream. When that happens you know it is big enough. Make no mistake about it, Walt Disney did not achieve his dream without hitting roadblocks along the way. Walt had to endure failure after failure before he was able to get a breakthrough. Snow White and the Seven Dwarfs was a make-it-or-break-it movie for Disney. He had everything riding on the success of that film.

One day Walt sent everyone to dinner and asked them to come back afterward as he had something to show them. When the crew returned, Walt acted out the entire movie as all the characters to get the buy-in from everyone on his vision. The rest is history. Disney went on to be a movie-making icon and build the largest entertainment enterprise on the planet.

Disney's visions for his theme park were so big, a part of it was not built until after he died in 1966. Epcot did not open until 1982, sixteen years after Walt's death. At the opening of Epcot, a reporter said to Walt's brother Roy, " *It's a shame Walt could not be here to see this.*" Roy replied, " *Walt did see it, and that's why you get to see it.*"

Are you dreaming big enough that your dreams won't even be finished in your lifetime? More importantly, do you have a plan to make your dream a reality? Most of us, if we're are honest with ourselves, have some amazing dreams and visions we intend to accomplish. The problem is we have no plan. A dream with no plan is just a vision. It becomes a should instead of a must.

Here is the part that is the most fun. The plan doesn't have to be perfect or final. It can constantly change and evolve as the process of the plan is being executed. All we have to do is get something down on paper that will allow us to take action **TODAY**! Then go and find a mentor or coach to hold us accountable for moving the plan forward.

In some instances, we call this the " *build the plane as we fly it approach.*" The important thing is to write down the plan and click the

GO button. It is impossible to see what is coming around the next corner. Waiting to take action until we have the perfect plan will freeze us into doing nothing. Get the fundamentals together, believe in the plan, and go learn what you don't know yet.

The Plan

"Success is the progressive realization of a worthy goal or ideal." —*Earl Nightingale*

Ok, so we are ready to put those dreams into a plan. Congratulations! This is the beginning of turning your dream into a reality. The first thing we want to do is start with the end in mind. What will your dream look like when it is completed? Write down your vision for when this dream is a reality. This oftentimes is the part that freezes people. There are two things all human beings desire, to look good and be right. We are so afraid about what others will think about us, or they will think our dream is stupid. What happens if I fail? How will it look if I take this chance and it doesn't work out?

There is no room in dreams for this type of negative thinking. There are two kinds of people, those who do and those who talk. If you are reading this book, then you're a doer. No matter what you intend to achieve or accomplish, there will always be haters. There will be the ones who talk and want to rain on your parade. News flash: the more you achieve, the bigger the hater's group will get. On the flip side, the more you achieve, those who support you will outnumber the hater's by a landslide.

The fear of failure falls into the category of wanting to be right. No one wants to fail at anything. I am going to share something with you that you can not tell anyone about. It is our little secret and I will know if you tell. *"Failure is the leading cause of success"*. I am just kidding about keeping a secret. Tell as many people this as you possibly can.

In our coaching company, we call it failing forward. A failure is only a failure if you don't learn anything. If you speak to anyone who ever accomplished a dream they will tell you that there is a lot of failing during the process. Failing is what helps people pivot and be able to turn the ship in the right direction so they can hit the goal.

Somewhere along the way, society made it unacceptable to fail. In doing so, it became more acceptable to not try and to settle for what life gives you, rather than to put yourself out there and fail along the way. This type of environment creates a belief system that says it's ok to dream, but not ok to fail. In the interview with Tyler Trainer, he talks at length about the process of failing and not stopping as a result of it.

Once you have your future dream written down and clear we can move on. Now we have to figure out how long that may take to accomplish. Ten years, five years, three years, or one year? However long it is going to take, we break it down over the next twelve months. What do I need to do monthly so that at the end of the twelve months I am well on my way? In this case, less is more. We are not looking to create a task list or checklist here that we are just going to check off. We are looking for two or three things monthly that will move the ball forward.

Then we move to weekly. The same principle, less is more. What are the two or three things weekly that need to happen to achieve the two or three things monthly? We then do the same daily, it is simply, what can I do in the next twenty-four hours that will help me win the day? Now go make your plan before you continue reading.

Limiting Beliefs

The belief system that stops us from moving forward is called limiting beliefs. Limiting beliefs are where dreams die. They will single-handedly destroy any hope of you having the dreams you want and deserve. These beliefs are responsible for most of our self-destructive behavior and freeze us from doing the things that we know we should do and won't.

When we are born we have zero limiting beliefs. When we are born we are only born with two natural fears. The fear of falling and the fear of loud noises. All other fears and beliefs that we acquire in our life are a result of our environment. Our parents are a huge influence in establishing our belief system. In a lot of cases, children acquire a high number of the beliefs their parents have just by proximity to them.

You may find yourself doing things now as an adult just because it's the way your parents always did it. It doesn't mean it is right or wrong, it is just the way you were led to believe it should be done. This falls under the saying, " *You are who you hang out with.*"

Someone shared a story with me once of a mother and daughter cooking a ham for a family holiday together, and before putting the ham in the oven the mother cut the end off. Her daughter asked why she always cut the end of the ham before putting it in the oven? Her mother said she didn't know she just saw her mother do it and just has always done it that way.

Later that afternoon when the family was all together, the daughter asked her grandmother, "why do you cut the end of the ham off before putting it in the oven?" The grandmother said there was no reason except years ago the ham was too big for her oven, so she had to cut it off for it to fit. There are now two generations of women who cut the end off their ham because they saw someone else do it. In this case, no harm no foul. While this does not fall into the same category as a limiting belief, It should make you think about some of the beliefs you have that have stopped you from getting what you want.

I remember as a child, I went to summer camp when I was about seven years old. The first day we had an activity at the pool and I had never been in a swimming pool before. I was standing in the shallow end and before I knew it I had lost my balance, slipped into the deep end, and didn't know how to swim. The lifeguard jumped in and rescued me. It scared the heck out of me and I decided not to go back to camp again. From that day until I was about 23 years old, I had the limiting brief that I just could not swim. I avoided swimming pools at all costs that could be over my head depth-wise. I missed out on so many pool parties and fun as a child because of this limiting belief.

When I moved to Florida in 2013, I decided that this fear had to end. I decided one day I was going to go into the pool and not get out until I at least felt comfortable floating around. Soon afloat became a doggy paddle, and before I knew it, I was swimming. It was so easy once I decided to just do it. Now I have a new belief. I can swim if I want to.

How many of your limiting beliefs have come from past experiences, or other people in your life that you spend a lot of time around? We all have these limiting beliefs and to think one day you will just wake up and poof they are gone goes against everything we know about how the brain works. We will run from pain before we ever go towards pleasure. It is the fight or flight response that we have in all of us as humans. We can't eliminate limiting beliefs overnight. What we can do is feel the fear and do it anyway. Doing it anyway will take far less energy than fighting with it. We need to empower ourselves to be able to see what fighting through the fear will get us on the other side. This is thinking with the end in mind.

When you can tie the joy and fulfillment of actually achieving your dream, it will motivate you to face these limiting beliefs head-on. It is ok to be afraid of what happens when you step outside your comfort zone. That fear you feel is what keeps us all alive. The final thing about limiting beliefs is don't go through it alone. Find a coach or a mentor that can walk side by side with you through the days when failure is imminent.

Limiting beliefs are not always obvious for us to see on our own. It often takes trained eyes and ears to be able to recognize and address these limiting beliefs. A coach or mentor will help you redirect these limiting beliefs into empowering beliefs, and put you in an accelerated momentum of growth.

The doers

Being a doer instead of a talker is what separates the ones who live the life they mapped out from the ones who just take what life gives them, and complain about nothing ever changing. These are people who come to Thanksgiving dinner and then suck the energy from the room by telling everyone why they don't have what they want and blame it on just about everyone else.

We all have people in our lives who frustrate us because they settle for so much less than they can be or have. Is it possible you're there now? The key to getting what we want is moving ahead every day. Even if it is just an inch forward, progress equals doing. There is nothing worse than feeling you are constantly on a hamster wheel. I don't just mean at work. Financially and personally, we get there too. Personal hamster wheels are the ones that hurt the most and sometimes become our least priority when attempting to move forward in other areas.

If you are not familiar with the term, " *Feeling like you on a hamster wheel,*" envision the daily life of a hamster. That little hamster is moving those legs like it is running for its life, exerting so much energy for what seems like hours. The hamster gets off the wheel and is in the same place it was the day before that and the day before that. This is a perfect example of mistaking movement for achievement. The hamster is moving and is taking total action. The problem is, the action isn't taking them anywhere.

We need to be sure that the actions we are doing are moving us forward. We need to take ownership of where we are based on the actions we have taken to get there. So many people blame others for not having what they want. They blame people like family, friends, co-workers, even the government. Not having what you want starts with you, and the steps you have taken to be a doer and not just a talker.

I am writing this chapter a few days after one of the United States of America's most controversial and divided Presidential elections in our nation's history with maybe the exception of the Civil War era. Almost one hundred fifty million Americans have voted in this election, which is a record. The results were almost split exactly down the middle.

The people who just talk instead of doing, blame the fact that people don't have what they want because of the person sitting in the White House or Congress. The only person responsible for your success or failures is you. Not your government, not your employer or employees, not your family... YOU.

Right now as I write this there are millions of people in complete panic mode that the outcome of this election will directly impact their ability to build their American Dream. Since the beginning of civilization, there has been constant change in leadership. Some for the better, some for the worse. What stays the same is that humans have two natural resources built in their programming if they choose to use them. They are resourceful and they have grit.

On the same morning that the media and the entire county were either celebrating a new president-elect or mourning over the end of a current president's era, one of the greatest stories in the history of sports and humanity happened. On Nov 7th, 2020, Chris Nikic, of Maitland Florida, became the very first person with Down Syndrome to become an Iron Man. No one had ever done this before. Not only had no one ever completed the race, no one with Down Syndrome had ever even attempted the race. So how do Chris and his family make this dream a reality? They seek out someone who has completed the race multiple times and was dedicated to the grueling training process to become an Iron Man.

An Ironman race consists of a 2.4-mile swim, followed by a 112-mile bicycle ride, and then you finish with running a full marathon. This must be completed in fewer than seventeen hours. There are only about 400,000 people in the entire world's history who have ever completed an Iron Man race. Not one of them with Down syndrome.

Do you think Chris and his family had limiting beliefs around this dream becoming a reality? Yes of course they did. He felt the fear and did it anyway. If you ever get to have a conversation with Chris, you will quickly realize he does not hold back on telling everyone his goals. With every person he tells, he is including them into his mission and reasons for doing this. In his get 1% better method, there is an enormous place for fear and limiting beliefs to seep in. Chis decided he would feel the fear and do it anyway. Chris received two Espy awards for this performance, he won the Male athlete with a disability award, and the crown jewel, the Jimmy V award.

The awards were a great tribute to this accomplishment, and if you ask Chris, it is not those awards that matter. The fact that he is putting *"Getting 1% better"* and inclusion on the map, is the most prestigious award he could have received. If what you are taking away from this story is that it is simply amazing that Chris finished that race, then you're missing the point. What is amazing is that Chris faced fear, limiting beliefs, and as you will read in his interview, major adversity during the race, and he did it anyway.

~ IV ~

THINKING FORWARD

"We keep moving forward, opening new doors, and doing new things because we're curious and curiosity keeps leading us down new paths."-Walt Disney

Thinking forward to seeing the end in mind, is where the rubber meets the road. I am not sure about you, but I am certainly guilty of getting stuck in the present moment. Doing the same thing over and over thinking we are moving towards something greater. Notice how I said *"thinking"* we are moving towards something greater. Without thinking forward and envisioning what that something greater is, we stay in the same old routine, talking about the same old things, and nothing ever changes.

Think of the movie with Bill Murray, *"Groundhog* Day." The Character Bill gets up every day, and it is the same day with the same interactions time after time after time. It gets to the point where he tries to kill himself multiple different ways, just to get somewhere different. This extreme measure doesn't even work, he just wakes up the morning after morning, doing the same old thing.

He finally realizes the opportunities that he has, by being able to anticipate what is coming next. He has lived this day over and over so many times he knows who he will meet and when he will meet them before they even show up. Once Bill realizes the advantages of anticipation he starts changing the days little by little.

He starts taking piano lessons and becomes an accomplished pianist. He also learns, through multiple failures, the likes and dislikes of the woman he is in love with. Bill is determined to win her over by using the repetition of the day to his advantage. Once Bill no longer sees the repetition of the day as a curse and sees it as an advantage, the story changes.

In the end, his vision comes true, and all the hard work and repetition pay off. Bill gets the girl and finally the next morning when they wake up, it is no longer February 2nd Groundhog Day. It is February 3rd and a day that Bill will be able to build on for months and years to come.

Although this is fiction, so many of these principles apply to the process of whatever journey you are on. Warren Buffet says, " *You can't feel the weight of a habit until it is too heavy to break.*" This applies to bad and good habits, and we all have both. The question is, do we recognize the good vs the bad, and can we do something about it?

The process is thinking about what you are looking to achieve and envisioning it when it is finished. This means taking yourself out of your current state of being and putting yourself into the future.

What will this look like?

Who will be around me?

What do I need to accomplish this year to move toward it?

Who do I have to become to accomplish this?

What daily habits are required?

These five questions will automatically allow your brain to take you there. What this process allows you to do is have the fun of casting the vision of your dream by looking forward, and breaking it down to what it will take every day to achieve it.

It is a simple but not easy process. Simple in nature and to memorize, and not so easy to always figure out who you need to become to accomplish your vision. This is when you can reflect on the next steps of your life. This process will help you find the systems and people to show you who you need to become.

By breaking down this process into its five parts it becomes less overwhelming:

Part 1: What will this look like?

We talked before about visionaries like Walt Disney and how he was able to envision things far beyond his years. If you were to envision yourself five to ten years down the road, what would things look like? Where do you live? What have you accomplished? What are you most proud of? All these known and specific questions will clarify who you have to be now, so you can have all of it in the future.

This exercise can be done alone or as a couple or a family. My wife and I spend a weekend every year together in October to be sure we are on track with what things need to look like. What is critical about checking in yearly on the long-term vision, is if we need to make any changes they are usually small ones that we can tweak quickly and get right back to it.

Part 2: Who will be around me?

This part can be used in the work-life, financial life, or personal life. In the interviews with Chris Nikic, David Berlant, and Tyler Trainer, you hear how they used part 2 in different ways. They all knew who they wanted around them by a certain time to achieve a certain goal. In all three cases, early on in their journey, they decided on who they would want around.

Tyler Trainer talks about for him to be able to take his company NXT Level Cuisine to the end of his vision, he needed more chefs in the kitchen. With David Berlant, it is all about "Who" he could surround himself with to hit his financial goals. Chris Nikic is all about inclusion and building a life of his own.

When we think about the who, that person may not be in our lives yet. We may have to seek them out over time. We can make a vision of the qualities that a person will have. Being able to draw the right people to you to achieve success and happiness is a carefully thought out process that will change everything in your life.

Ask these 3 questions when choosing who will be around you:

Who needs to be around you?

Why them, what about their journey causes you to want them in your life?

What qualities do they have?

Part 3: What do I need to accomplish this year to move forward?

Twelve months seems like a long time until it isn't. As we get older and more productive, our years fly by faster and faster. We make goals in January, and before you know it Spring is here. Summer consumes us with vacations and day trips to the beach. Before you know it, you are staring at the fourth quarter wondering where the year went.

Planning specifics on what you need to accomplish in the upcoming or current year is what speeds us towards our " forward-thinking" goals. The keyword there is **specific**. Just like we spoke about "the why" in Chapter 2, less is more. Having two or three things to focus on, allows you to focus energy in the places that matter.

Part 4: Who do I have to become to accomplish this?

This question goes along with finding out what skills, behaviors, and characteristics you would need to adapt or improve on to reach your ultimate goal? When we ask. " Who do I have to become?" it is not an insult to who we currently are. It is a process of self-reflection to see where we can improve to get what we want. When we find out who we have to become, we can start the journey of putting it all together.

Think of someone you admire or look up to who has already accomplished what you want. Take a deep hard look at them, and then take the same look at yourself. Say to get what you want, you need to increase your leadership skills. Ok perfect, now all you have to do is get some leadership training. That can be done through reading books, attending seminars, or simply getting a mentor or coach.

Once you have identified the gap in who you are in these areas, and who you want to become, the rest is as simple as being resourceful enough to go and find the answers. Often people know exactly what they want, and lack the willingness to become who they need to be so they can have it.

Part 5: What daily habits are required?

Now that you have identified who you need to become to get what you want, the next step is to develop the habits of that person. Developing new habits takes time and effort. Many of us with big dreams fail to acknowledge that. Breaking old bad habits is a million times more challenging.

So if breaking an old habit is so much more challenging than developing a new one, why do most people start with breaking old habits, instead of just creating new ones? In so many cases, when new habits are identified we automatically focus on bad habits we need to break. If we reverse the process and start developing the new habit first, the old habits can be phased out naturally.

Let's take the goal of wanting to get into better shape. The first thing someone might say is, " I need to stop eating fatty foods." That would be trying to break an old habit, which we know is much harder than creating a new one. Instead of focusing only on cutting out fatty foods, this person could say, " I am going to start going to the gym."

Focusing on the new habit of going to the gym gives you a positive outlook on attacking this goal. In the process of going to the gym and working hard to get into better shape, something magical happens. The fatty food habit starts to become less desirable. Simply because you are spending so much energy at the gym to burn a few calories, you don't want to eat two bowls of ice cream and reverse all the hard work you just accomplished.

The next time you decide on a goal, start with the new habit first for 60 days and see how many of the old bad habits just naturally fade away. You will be surprised at how easy that will be. For the bad ones that don't naturally fade away, we can focus on the time and energy it will take to break that habit.

Breaking the chains

"We change our behavior when the pain of staying the same becomes greater than the pain of changing. Consequences give us the pain that motivates us to change."
— **Dr. Henry Cloud & Dr. John Townsend**

The chains of habits are brutal, especially the ones that don't bring us any immediate and obvious harm. We have no incentive to make a change because our livelihood does not appear to be at risk. Even the habits we have that are putting us in grave danger are sometimes too much for people to overcome. Take smokers, for example. For the past sixty-plus years there has been a warning on the packaging of cigarettes explaining the dangers of smoking. If that doesn't do it for you, we have all watched loved ones die a very painful death from the effects of smoking. Even still for some, that is not enough to make the change.

It is simply pain vs pleasure. When you smoke at the age of 25, for the most part, you feel no immediate danger. You can still run and jump and keep up with everyone else. You are, however, smart enough to know and have seen what a habit of smoking will do to you in 20 to 30 years. The pain of what may happen in the future is not immediate enough to outway the pleasure now. As a 25-year-old, you feel you can stop anytime and in plenty of time before it kills you. Until you don't. Until the addiction is so ingrained in your daily life it is almost impossible to stop in time.

This is a severe example, and there are thousands more we can use that end the same way. NOT EVER GETTING WHAT YOU WANT! What we do daily compounds and becomes our destiny. Our daily activities, personally and professionally outweigh any other thing in the process of the five questions I lay out in this chapter.

Breaking the chains of old habits can take months. It is not as simple as saying, *"I am going to quit smoking, start working out, eat better, prospect daily for new clients in my business."* None of that. That is just the beginning of the process. Starting what you should or would like to do is just the first step. Replacing the old habit with the new and scheduling it, is the real magic. It is not always enough to say what habits you want to start or stop. We have to put these actions in our calendars so the calendar matches our intentions.

Does my calendar match my vision?

The numbers 1,440 and 86,400 should become your new favorite numbers. What makes these two numbers so important is they are bigger numbers than most people are ever asked to remember. These are the number of minutes and seconds in a single day. They are the most fixed numbers in the world, and the only numbers, besides the 365 day year and 24 hour day, that are international.

At the time this book is being written there are just under 7.7 billion people in the world. Only about 330 million of them live in the United States. So that means you have something in common with every person who has achieved what you wish to achieve, and something in common with people who have achieved more than you can even imagine achieving. That something is time.

This is all we get guys. We need to take advantage of every minute or second possible. The idea that we will get to it tomorrow is a myth. You won't get to it tomorrow, or the next day, or the next day. Tomorrow will not come unless you take action. If 90-year-old Warren Buffet is worth 85 billion dollars getting the same amount of time we do each day, we know what is possible.

If you read or listen to anything Warren Buffet has to say about his success, it is all about creating empowering habits one day at a time. What will you do? Will procrastination set in, or will paralysis by analysis set in and freeze you? I challenge you to take advantage of the time you are given daily. Go build great businesses and relationships so that you become the chess player and not the chess piece.

~ V ~

YOU DON'T KNOW WHAT YOU DON'T KNOW

" People who don't know what they don't know and then follow a system to learn what they don't know, win big."
-Terry Gurno

When we think about our plan for the future, we may have a picture of what we want it to look like and still have no idea how we are going to get there. What we know is when our dream is achieved how we will feel. Or do we? We would like to think we know exactly how our lives will look once all of our hopes and dreams are achieved, but we don't know what we don't know.

Think about when you started the job or career you have now. Look back at where you started and compare that to where you are now, you are much better at what you do. You have evolved in the role over time by learning from others, making mistakes, and repeating the job day, after day. This is no different when chasing a dream of starting something new. We can't be frozen in place because we don't know everything there is to know upfront.

Over the years, I have coached hundreds of real estate professionals. When many get into the business, they focus on getting everything perfect before they start the process of acquiring clients. They want to perfect the exact things to say, the perfect marketing materials, and the perfect presentation. The biggest challenge with this strategy is that you perfect the perfect presentation and language for a client you don't have. Until you have gone on several consultation appointments, how will you know what you need to prepare for?

Others come out of the gates swinging. They start with networking, contacting the people who know and trust them, and along the way learning what they need to do to get and close an appointment. They align themselves with people who can help them make the perfect marketing and presentation. This strategy works much more often than not, simply because the sales associate is learning in the field every day what they didn't know yesterday.

Which scenario do you think finds the most success in the business? Scenario two by a landslide. These folks understand that in the real estate industry, talking to people who talk back to you is the quickest way to build a successful business. Attempting to make everything perfect is the ultimate failure.

I have been involved in the real estate industry now for almost fifteen years, and my presentation, marketing, and language of sales are still far from perfect. I am much better now than I was on day one. Imagine over the past fifteen years if I said I was not going to start pursuing clients until I had everything perfect. I would have been out of business by year two.

In my first year in business for myself, the economy was just beginning the great recession. People's homes lost value overnight, and their equity was plummeting three percent month over month for about eighteen months. Being a rookie, I did not know any better. I didn't know any other markets, good or bad. All I knew was what was happening in front of me at that moment.

In the five years prior, real estate sales professionals did not need to do much to make money. Prices were continuing to rise and home loans were just being given away with little or no proof of documentation. People thought that the market was just going to continue this way forever. They didn't know what they didn't know, or did they? Was there evidence that there was going to be a market correction based on history?

Of course, there was. Historical trends always show what goes up must come down. Since the 1920s, we can go back and look at all the trends and study them. What it shows you is that things never continue to go up. Whether it goes up gradually or aggressively, it will not stay there. Sure over the long term, even with market corrections, markets trend up. Homes are worth way more than they were in the 1920s, and there have been many corrections along those 100 years that brought markets to their knees for some time.

In my first year in real estate sales, it was like a massacre at the brokerage firm I was working for. One person after another failed to anticipate what was coming and lost their business, this was most prevalent in the ones who were less than five years in the business. It had always been a hot market for them, so they felt they never needed to be strategic and learn how to go out and get business. All they needed for the past five years was a cell phone and vehicle and they could make a ton of money. One day that stopped and 99% of the sales force was unprepared. Most left the business for other careers.

This could have been the best thing I witnessed in my career. If I had decided to enter the business just one year earlier this could have been me. I learned quickly that the fastest path to winning in a business I knew nothing about was to find someone to mentor me, and quickly. This was a small brokerage as it was, and not too far into my time there only a few remained selling full time.

The brokerage had a mentoring program. For your first three transactions, they would set you up with someone who had found success to help you get started. In theory, this program was a great idea, and in some cases worked well. The challenge was that the mentor assigned to me had only been in the business for two years. He meant well, and for some of the paperwork and presentation systems, it worked perfectly for me. With his lack of experience in a down market, however, it was not going to get me to the level I needed. I had to attach myself to someone who had seen something like this before.

My search for this, believe it or not, lasted for two years. I floundered for two years, making just enough sales to put food on the table. That was not what I signed up for. I left the construction world to pursue this career, and in the construction world, I was doing much more than putting food on the table.

Around the time I was about to quit and go back to construction, I started to see a trend. One by one, some of the biggest players in this brokerage, people who had been there for years, started to leave. They weren't getting out of the business. They all left to go to the same brokerage right next door. One of them was even the brother of my current broker.

When that happened, I had to inquire about the why. I met the broker of this new brokerage. What I discovered was this company specialized in helping agents that didn't know what they didn't know. They gave their agents the models and systems to be able to thrive whether the market was up or down. They thought that there are no bad markets, just bad mindsets. They believed there was an opportunity in every market if you learn where to look.

BINGO!!! This was it, this was exactly what I needed, and didn't know I needed. I had just completed my first three years in the business full of doubt, and being led down a road that was going to bankruptcy. In my first year with this new company, I did more sales than my previous 3 years combined. It was simply unbelievable how the same person who had the same amount of time in the day for the past three years, could make such a turnaround in fewer than twelve months.

There were models and systems I was given to follow, and even more importantly than that, there were multiple people in the office who had been through a down market before. All I had to do was ask anyone in the office for help when I had a question or a problem, and I had answers. Over a decade later, I still consult with the same group of sales associates about my businesses. I built so many relationships far beyond real estate in this type of culture, and I was even fortunate enough to meet my wife in this group.

Be open to what you don't know

For some of us as we get older, we are less and less open to hearing where we can improve, and to learn new things. Some have a mindset that by a certain age they should already know how to make things happen, or they should be at a certain place in life. This type of mindset can stunt the growth you are looking for. It robs you of taking advantage of the mentor and coaching experience.

If you make yourself vulnerable enough to seek out a mentor or coach, you owe it to yourself and to the mentor or coach to be open to all new ways of doing things and to new ideas. Sometimes when we get a mentor and coach they will share systems or ideas with us that may not be in our comfort zone. This is when a real decision needs to be made for yourself. You have sought out this person, and they have shared what contributes to their success, and you say, " *That doesn't seem like me."*

The decision you will need to make here is whether or not the goal you are pursuing is worth the effort of going outside your comfort zone to achieve it. So many people waste their time in coaching and with a mentor by being unwilling to make the necessary changes to get the results they are looking for. If that is you that is fine, just stop what you are doing and find something else you are willing to achieve because this goal will not happen.

Don't spend months and years banging your head against the wall with a mentor or a coach if you are just going to try to reinvent the wheel inside your comfort zone. You will know in a matter of days if you are coachable and do what is necessary or not to achieve your goal. Sometimes when you look behind the curtain and see what it takes to be successful in this goal, it goes against your values or beliefs. This is ok, just find a new goal and restart the process. No one should go against their values or beliefs to make a goal happen. Simply take a moment and reset yourself on a new track. If it's not a matter of values and beliefs and you simply just don't want to go outside your comfort zone to grow, then that is a different story altogether.

I remember one of the first things a mentor told me in real estate when I changed brokerages was to get a role play partner and practice my scripts every day. First off, I had been in the business for three years and never heard of scripts. This person wanted me to practice saying what I was going to say to a client when I called them every day. So many things were running through my mind. What if I sound terrible? It would be so embarrassing to screw up in front of another colleague.

I expressed my concerns to my mentor and she said this in a very sweet and loving tone, *"Would you rather practice with me or practice with your clients?"* Whoa, that was a hit right in the face. I never thought of it that way. Every time I was going on an appointment I was practicing with them. She said, *"If you want to get more people to say yes to working with you, then you need to be better prepared."*

This may not sound like groundbreaking advice to you, and we don't know what we don't know. This one piece of advice changed everything for my career moving forward. It also took me completely out of my comfort zone. I have been roleplaying now for over a decade and still am not 100% comfortable with it. I still don't like the way I sound when I do it. At the end of the day, all that matters is being prepared for the opportunity.

Take a look at where you are now. How can this story relate to something you're striving for at the moment? Ask yourself, *" Is there something I have been advised to do, that I just have not implemented yet, that could change everything?"* If the answer is yes, you have to take one of two actions.

1. Implement the idea immediately
2. Get a new goal

Number one is self-explanatory. If you know you need to take action, then surround yourself with the right support team and go for it. If you just won't for one reason or another take that action then just make a new goal with ingredients that you will take action on. If you have not been advised to do something that can move you forward, ask your mentor or coach what that something could be.

What to look for in my mentor or coach

Finding the right mentor or coach gives us the confidence to take action when we don't know what we don't know. Picking the person or persons has a process just like everything else. Picking the right person will push you forward faster than you ever thought possible, and picking the wrong person could set you back decades. Here are a few must-haves when searching for this person.

Must-haves:

- A history of success in their life.
    - Not necessarily in the industry or dream, you're looking to achieve.
    - If this person has a history of achieving their goals they have a system you can learn from.
- Will not let you off the hook.
    - If this person will not hold you accountable for the plan of what you said you would do, then they are the wrong person.
- Will make your goals their goals.
    - The correct coach or mentor wants to create a sacred partnership with you.
    - They will be just as excited about your goals as you are.

Before you turn the page, create a list of places you can find your mentor or coach. Understanding that a mentor and coach are two different things, and it's preferred to have both to make major strides. A mentor is someone who can lead by example and show you the how and why of it all. A coach is a partner who shares models and systems and holds you accountable for the actions you have committed to. Now make your list and start reaching out to interview your next mentor and coach.

~ VI ~

TAKING IMMEDIATE ACTION

"Either you run the day or the day runs you."
— Jim Rohn

Procrastination is something we are all guilty of at some point or another in our lives. The definition of procrastination is, *"The action of delaying or postponing something."* The definition could also read, *"the killer of my dreams and goals."* As human beings, we naturally take the path of least resistance and accomplish the easy quick tasks first. We say things like *"Tomorrow is another day."* The phrase, *"tomorrow is another day,"* has got to be the most non-productive phrase in any language.

It serves no purpose to put off until tomorrow what we have committed to do today, especially the things that move us closer to accomplishing our dreams and goals. Garth Brooks recorded a song, *"If tomorrow never comes."* In this song, he talks about how what we put off until tomorrow has now become today. If tomorrow never comes, are you any closer to achieving what you desire today than you were yesterday?

For a great number of people, the answer is no. We go through our day and check things off of our list that is familiar and comfortable. We push off the things that are outside our comfort zone and say, *"I will do it later today, or tomorrow."* In earlier chapters, we started to put your dreams and goals into a plan. If immediate action is not taken all you have is a plan, that has very little chance of being executed if immediate action is not taken within twenty-four hours. I suggest twenty-four hours because it is fresh in your mind. You have the most energy and excitement around it right now. The longer we procrastinate and allow time to fly by, the less likely we will ever take action at all. Time stops for no one, so now is a good time to take action on your plan?

Envision a snowball rolling down a hill, it becomes bigger and bigger as it builds momentum. It did not start as an unstoppable force. The ball started as a little ball of snow that was fragile and barely noticed. This is what the minutes following putting your plan together look like. Your plan is fragile and can't come to life without you making the first move. You have a very limited amount of time to start the execution of that plan, before the habit of procrastination sets in and it never even has a chance to become a reality.

One of my passions is antique cars and hot rods. Over the years, I have had my fair share of them, and most were projects that needed some TLC along the way. I remember one car in particular that I believed didn't have a motor powerful enough for my liking. My friends and I decided we would go and get a used engine that had the power we needed and make the swap.

I had no experience in engine swapping, and my friends had only a little more than I. We decided to give it a go and I called around and found the engine that would work. We all got together one Saturday and removed the old engine, and of course, in the process of doing this, we made no diagram or took any pictures of how it was supposed to go back together. We disconnected the transmission and clutch, pulled a few bolts from the frame, and in a matter of a couple of hours, that old slow engine was out of the car.

Now, all we had to do was put the new one in. Simple right? NOPE! None of us had ever used an engine hoist before. Pulling it out was one thing, now we had to get this bigger engine to fit and not crush anything or anyone. In lowering the engine into its location the engine hit the heater box and crushed it. No heater box equals no heat by the way. After that, we were able to get the engine into position and secure it to the frame. The heavy lifting was done and my friends and I decided to call it a day and everyone went home. My dream now was to get this car back on the road and to cruise nights where it belonged. All that was left to do was to hook up the transmission and clutch and off I would go.

Remember when I said we documented nothing and took no pictures? Well for someone who had never put these things back together before there were more pieces than holes to put them in. I said I would do some research and ask around on the best way to get these pieces hooked back up. Days, weeks, and months went by and life got in the way, including working every day and family obligations. To make a long story short, that car never saw the road again. It just became a project I procrastinated on and never got back to. To this day, almost two decades later, I still wonder what would have happened if I had just followed through on what I wanted, even if I had just taken it a little at a time.

Procrastination is the " *Killer of dreams and goals,"* and I will believe that until the day I die. The story of my car project is just one of many personal examples I can share of disappointment I have had in my life, simply as a result of procrastinating. How many stories do you have? Who is no longer in your life or what opportunities have you missed because you didn't take action NOW?

The twenty-four-hour rule is not just for implementing your plan to accomplish your dreams and goals. It is for everything. Anytime you attend a seminar, workshop, read a book, or receive advice, whatever it is you learned that you wish to implement in your own life, the first step needs to be taken in the first twenty-four hours. The twenty-four-hour rule is the kryptonite for procrastination.

The twenty-four-hour rule

People love to educate themselves on how to push to the next level in whatever it is they want to do. In the U.S. alone, corporations and individuals combined to spend over eighty-five billion dollars a year on education and self-development. That number increases year over year as people are searching for that secret pill to push them over the top. Hoping that with every event they attend or every book they read, there will be an answer there that will make an easier path for them.

Education without implementation is just entertainment. Just reading the book or attending the training doesn't accomplish anything. It is what is done with the knowledge that can create lasting change. When you read a book, attend a seminar, or listen to a PODcast, do you write down notes on action steps you will take as soon as it is over to implement what you learned?

Most of us live out my car engine story, time after time. We have great intentions to do just what we learned, and when we do it will change everything. Then life happens. People get busy, your time gets divided, and you end up with the smartest bookshelf and notebook on the planet.

The next time you are at training or reading a book like this one, and want to create lasting change, try the 24-hour rule. Here is the process.

1. Look at your notes and pick three things you can implement.
2. Make one of the three something you can do short-term.
3. Make one something that will take a little longer.
4. Make one that is a long-term vision.
5. Execute the first action item in the next twenty-four hours.

The reason I say pick three things to implement is that when we attempt to implement more than that, we implement nothing. Overwhelm sets in and we never get started. When attending a class or seminar, or even reading a book, there are so many things that can get you excited and that you want to get started on. Narrowing them to three things that you must do increases our chances of success.

Making one of them a short-term goal will allow you to get started and see results very quickly. It doesn't have to be an over-the-moon goal, just something that you have to take action on immediately to see results toward the overall vision of your goal. The short term would be something that can be completed in six months or fewer.

The second thing you picked to implement would be a little longer plan, something six to eighteen months to complete. Oftentimes, you may have to build a new habit to complete this action, or add someone to your life or business, and would take more time. It is ok to take action on something starting now, knowing you may not see the fruits of the action for months to come.

The third thing would be a long-term plan. Something two-plus years away to be completed. We live in a results-now type society, and a lot of people will not take action on something that they won't see results in for years. We see this in the business world all the time. A business owner will start a plan and do it one or two times and quit because they feel they are not getting the results they hoped in the short term.

There are many things in business and in life that just take longer for you to see the results. Have you ever invested, and in the short term very little or no returns were made? Then all of a sudden one day you look, and that investment is worth so much more than it was a few years ago. Some things take longer to blossom than others.

That is why the process of implementing something now to achieve success for something down the road is so important. If all we do is look for the immediate result or feeling, we never plant seeds that will grow our future down the road. Leaving a class, conference, or finishing a book, and taking action on all three plans in the first twenty-four hours ensures success.

Taking action within twenty-four hours moves you from a plan to a reality. If you take action in the first twenty-four hours of making a plan, you are 80% more likely to achieve it. It doesn't have to be a big thing. Just something that starts that snowball coming down the hill so it can grow from there.

Breaking the procrastination pattern

No one ever says, *"I am so glad I procrastinated on that."* Everyone talks about procrastination as a pattern they would like to break.

It usually ends up on your New Year's resolution list and never makes it past January fifteenth. Just reading this book, or putting the words, *"Stop procrastinating"* on a list is not going to have it magically stop.

In Chapter 4 we went deep into the process of creating new habits and fading out old ones. I singled out procrastination specifically because of how damaging it is to everyone who struggles with it. When you look at someone who constantly procrastinates, you often see a person who is also in a constant state of suffering.

They have missed out on experiences, relationships, adventures, and income, simply because, *"Tomorrow was another day."* It is a myth to think we will never procrastinate on another thing as long as we live. The purpose of this conversation is to break the cycle of procrastinating on all the things that are a priority in your life.

Here is a process to get started on your new journey immediately:

1. Start with day one and take action on something today.
2. Time block one hour per day for this action.
3. Tell someone else your plan so they can help hold you accountable weekly, preferably a mentor or coach.

When we start a new journey, the end date of that journey is undetermined. The start date, however, must be determined and booked on your calendar. There is a saying, *"The best time to plant a tree was ten years ago, and the next best time is right now."* When we are building for our future, we are constantly planting trees along the way. The more trees we plant, the bigger our lives become.

It is one thing to say we are going to start a new journey. Scheduling it is another. We all attempt to cram as much into our days and weeks as we possibly can, so we can accomplish as much as we can. By doing this we don't always leave room on the calendar to start anything new. As soon as you put the action steps for your new journey on the calendar, it becomes real.

The last part of the process is telling someone else what you plan to accomplish. When we share our goals and get some accountability around them, our success rate is extraordinary. Oftentimes we are afraid to share these things with other people in case we fall short. That is exactly why we should do it.

No one wants to fall short on what they say they will do. Just a simple thing like telling someone will motivate you to push through on the hard days. I recommend a mentor or coach, so you have the true experience of accountability throughout the process.

Now you are ready to take procrastination out of your life for good and become more on purpose about your dreams and goals. These principles are simple, but not easy. Falling forward in these in the short term is part of the process. No one goes to the gym for one time and says, *"I'm in shape."* It takes many days in a row of making it a priority before becomes a habit. You will know it is a habit when it feels weird not to do it.

~ VII ~

BEING SPREAD TOO THIN

*" Don't try to be good at everything, don't spread your-
self so thin that you accomplish nothing; rather, pick a
few things and do them well. Excel in those areas and
you'll excel in life." -- Rachel Van Dyken*

There are 8,760 hours every year, 730 hours in a month, 168
hours in a week, and 24 hours every day. That is it, no more and no
less. For years, I have been trying to push for a day in between Saturday and Sunday to make a long weekend and to no avail. This is
all we get so we need to make the best of the time we have.

Watching how people delegate their time truly fascinates me. It
is the number one issue entrepreneurs struggle with in achieving
success. Even the highest of achievers fail to take into account the
amount of time there is to work with. They find out in the end,
that being busy and achieving actual results are two very different
things.

What fascinates me about time is the amount we have each day.
It is the only thing we know for certain. In life, we can never anticipate everything that will happen to us. Take the year 2020. We
were going on living the way we had been for years. Then in March,
complete change happened.

In March of 2020, the world was completely shut down by a global pandemic. Covid-19 disrupted almost all lives and businesses. People were forced to stay home and shut down an economy that was booming. Many businesses that were decades old were forced to shut their doors for good. None of it was any fault of their own. One day business was thriving and a few months later, closed. Nothing is certain.

Nothing that is, except time. When you plan your year, month, week, and day, we need to take a look at how fixed time is into consideration. Most of us see it as a challenge, that there just isn't enough time. It is the opposite. It is the only certain advantage we have when planning.

When you pre-plan your week or day in advance you can see if the calendar matches the goals. Are the things to be completed adding up to more time than is allowed? Living in time blocks is hardly ever exciting, but the results are. Results come from figuring out how long a goal will take, and being sure the time blocked on your calendar for it is concrete.

Does your calendar match your goals?

Every Sunday evening, I plan my week. I look at the seven days ahead and write down all the things that need to happen this week to achieve the success I am looking for. This includes business and personal. Almost always, people schedule their business appointments first and cram the personal stuff in later.

When you do this nine times out of ten you never make it to the personal stuff at all. The first thing I do every Sunday is block out my personal time. Time with my daughter, my wife, and for myself. Then when this is blocked out, we can start on the business appointments.

Once you have your personal and work time set, look at your calendar and count how much white unused space is left. It should be twenty-five to fifty percent of your day. This allows you to have flexibility when life happens to you.

Never in my life have I ever gone through an entire month where a few of life's surprises haven't reared their ugly head. It is going to happen, and going through your month thinking it is always going to be perfect is delusional. Again, why fight the one constant and certainty we have... time.

Let's say on Monday from 8:00 a.m. to 10:00 a.m. you have time scheduled to prospect for new business for the month. Monday morning your child wakes up with a fever and needs to see a doctor. This was not scheduled and it was unforeseen, and completely out of your control.

You are thinking, *"I did not plan for this and I need to contact new prospective clients."* If you, add enough white space into your calendar then you are planning for it. All you have to do when this happens is just move the prospecting time block to one of the white spaces you have already allocated for that week.

You get to go back and attend to your sick child and not have to give the business side of your world a second thought. This is a very powerful tool that is underutilized by a huge portion of the population. Having a sick child is stressful, but there is no need to stress about the time it is costing you at the same time. When we are in control of our calendar and have the space to move things around, amazing things happen.

You feel less stressed already because you're setting yourself up for success. One question I get a lot is, *"What happens if I don't use the white space that day?"* That is completely up to you. You can double down on the action steps you have written down to achieve your goals. Or you can take time for yourself and that's great too.

Another question I get a lot is, *"What happens if I enter everything I need to do into my calendar and there is no white space? If there is white space it is not anywhere near twenty-five to fifty percent."* The answer is, you have too many obligations. Somewhere in your life, you need to delegate some of your responsibilities elsewhere. Otherwise, you will keep chasing this uphill battle and never have enough time.

A process that has helped people create more white space is to start their calendar over again from scratch.

- First, we take any calendar template and start with all-white spaces.
- Then we fill in all the personal time we need for ourselves, our family, spiritual time, and our health.
- The next step is to fill in the most important money-making activities in your job or business.
- At this point count how much white space is left. If it is more than 25%, adding more obligations is acceptable
- Once your calendar is 25% white space, stop.
- There will most likely be extra items that have not made it onto your calendar. These are the things that we either delegate to someone else or stop committing to.

Embrace the White Space

Staring at a calendar that has multiple white spaces in it for some can be terrifying. Most of the time when I have the opportunity to look at someone's calendar I see spaces filled back to back to back. From the time they wake up until the time they go to bed, there is no stopping. There is also no room for error.

Let's just say you have appointments booked back to back with no space in between from 9:00 am until 3:00 pm. Your first appointment shows up on time and all is well, but your 10:00 am appointment is running fifteen minutes late. Now, what do we do? We have no room for error for someone to be behind schedule. Now because this appointment is running late, your entire day is going to be running late.

This can cause an enormous amount of stress. In this scenario, there could be a chance to make up the fifteen minutes if you just shorten your lunch and just eat fast. Now the time we have scheduled to recharge the batteries with food and rest is gone. We have sacrificed it because someone else was running late in their day.

This can all be avoided by just scheduling two or three blocks of white spaces throughout the day. That way when unexpected things come up throughout the day, there is already time scheduled to get us back on track. On those days when things are going great and the white spaces are not needed to catch up, you have them there to do whatever you wish to do with them.

This process is something that will take practice to get used to. Once you do, it is a complete life changer. I remember watching David Berlant start his process of wanting to be an Iron Man. In his interview in this book, he shares his struggles, and the time commitment he made to the training.

There were so many habits that he was training for besides the training of his body for the race. He was training for the habit of waking up at 5 a.m. to swim before work, and he was protecting his time in the afternoons to get the run-in after work. The most difficult habit he had to train for was to know when to schedule the days to just let the body rest and recover from all the workouts to prevent injury.

That was the white space for him. Telling himself he wanted to be faster and stronger every day and at the same time, take a break and recharge. For someone who is on a mission to be the very best at what they do, the white space feels like a waste of time. Stopping and scheduling time to do nothing seems counterproductive. Some feel lazy taking advantage of the white space.

Have you ever found yourself with extra time on your hands and just felt lost and didn't know what to do with it? That is a pre-conditioned feeling that comes from a belief system that was ingrained in us by someone else. You think that it is so much you could be doing, that taking a moment for you is unproductive laziness. That has become a common issue in the western world.

In many parts of Europe, businesses close in the afternoon for a few hours to allow themselves to enjoy the day. I remember walking around Italy a few years ago wondering, *"Where are all the people?"* I still am not sure where they were, but I know for certain they were not working. Pretty much the whole city just shut down for a couple of hours.

I am aware this practice may not be practical if you live in the United States. For them, it is a good use of scheduled white space. They just chose to schedule their white space all at once. It didn't make them any less successful or lazy. It does allow them to recharge and give the best of themselves for the remainder of the day.

Someone else's example of a productive week doesn't have to be yours. The blank calendar template is like the blank canvas that you can make into anything you wish it to be. You can put your personal, professional, and white space anywhere that fits your life and helps you get the result you are looking for. Nothing will bring you closer to achieving results than having complete control of your calendar.

If this is striking a nerve with you then put down this book and go make your calendar right now. As I said here, this is the single most important piece of any goal or dream you wish to accomplish. So just start now! Play with it until you find the formula that works for you. If you make your calendar and you realize it needs tweaking, then tweak it. You are in control of your destiny the minute you control your time.

~ VIII ~

WHERE'S YOUR PARADE?

" Remember to celebrate milestones as you prepare for the road ahead."
-Nelson Mandela

Being originally from New England, from the years 2001 - 2020, as sports fans, we had a lot to celebrate. In 2001 our "Golden Boy," Tom Brady came on the scene and led the Patriots to their first-ever Super Bowl Championship. They would go on to win six total Super Bowls in the span of those nineteen years in nine Super Bowl appearances.

In 2004, the Boston Red Sox won their first World Series in eighty-six years. After many heartbreaking years, this team was able to overcome incredible odds. They got past the New York Yankees, after trailing in that series three games to none in the American League Championship Series. They then went on to the World Series and swept the St. Louis Cardinals four games in a row. They would go on to win again in 2007, 2013, and 2018.

In 2008, the Boston Celtics with the Big 3, Paul Pierce, Kevin Garnett, and Ray Allen, won their first NBA Finals, since 1986. After the glory days of the 1960s and 1980's dynasties, the Celtics could not bring a championship back to Boston until 2008. These three players were and still are idolized in all of New England.

The Boston Bruins in 2011 brought home the Stanley Cup for the first time since the Bobby Orr days of 1972. With the goaltending of Tuukka Rask, and leadership of Patrice Bergeron, Zdeno Chara, David Krejci, and Brad Marchand, the Bruins defeated the Vancouver Canucks in seven games. The New England area big four sports teams brought home twelve major championships in eighteen years.

So what makes this so significant to a book about processes? Everything! For starters, when your professional sports team wins a major championship, we celebrate to the fullest. We glue ourselves to the T.V. every time our sports teams are in a playoff or tournament as if our life depended on it. Why don't we do this in our own lives or businesses? As human beings celebrating both our big and minor victories for the most part doesn't even cross our minds.

Children celebrate everything all of the time. When you watch a child, they get excited over just walking across the room sometimes. Children allow their imagination to run wild and even the adults to celebrate with them. At some point in our lives, we lost the habit of celebrating.

A few years back, I was the director of sales for one of the most successful real estate organizations in Central Florida. David Berlant, who you will meet later in the book, was also a leader on that team. Dan Grieb, who you will also meet later, was the owner of that team. We had a goal that year of hitting 450 sold homes. That would mean we would have helped 450 families find a place they would call home, and take one step closer to the "American Dream".

The most this team in the years prior had ever reached together was just over 350 units. We knew we were going to have to make a plan and be willing to do things that we had never done before to achieve 450 homes sold. We as a team made the plan of what the year would look like. We broke it down to what we would have to do weekly and even daily to hit the goal.

Our leadership team knew from past experiences that we had to focus on achieving little milestones to keep the team engaged and not lose focus on hitting a goal that was twelve months away. People have a hard time staying motivated on one goal that is that big, so we broke it down into chunks. We got the team together and asked them individually how many units they would like to close to hit their personal and financial goals. Each team member turned in their numbers and their collective number was closer to 475 units. This was 175 units more than the team had ever accomplished.

We all figured out that each team member needed to make one new appointment per day, five days per week. Based on the conversion ratio from each team member of 65%, we would write enough contracts per week that times fifty-two weeks, we would make the 475 transactions. The leadership team hired a coach that was known for helping teams bridge the gap from where they are to where they want to be. We set up a weekly call to report our progress and get guidance on our leadership. We had a scorecard that we had to fill out to keep track of the whole team's numbers.

In January and February, we were able to report that we were at, or exceeded our goals as a team. As the leadership team, we felt like we may smash the goal at this pace. What we failed to acknowledge was the team's engagement, and to reward the team for the job they were doing. March was the first time we reported numbers short of what we had committed to. No one on the leadership team was excited to get on the call with our coach to talk about not hitting our number. We entered our numbers into the scorecard and braced for the accountability that would come our way. To our surprise, our coach only asked how many times in the past twelve weeks we had celebrated the wins along the way with the team.

The answer was zero. We had failed to acknowledge all the hard work and effort they had been putting in. Our coach encouraged us to celebrate with the time weekly and monthly. Weekly acknowledgment at the team meetings and monthly team get-togethers were very important. Our coach promised that with little wins along the way, the team would stay engaged together as a unit.

The rest of the year the team would either exceed the goal or come very close to the goal each month. Our coach continued to encourage us even when we came up just short of the goal, to celebrate what we accomplished as a team. That year we finished the year with just over 400 homes closed. Although it was short of the numbers we had set out to accomplish at the beginning of the year, it was so much more than we had ever done. At the end of that year, we were used to celebrating and we had one heck of a party.

It is so important on our journey to continue to celebrate the little victories along the way. Until we can celebrate our victories as much as we celebrate the wins of our favorite sports teams, we will never truly appreciate the strides we are making. We will lose focus and let life get in the way of what we truly want, and we will celebrate the accomplishments of others instead. Once a week, take an hour and truly celebrate what wins you had that week.

Celebration is appreciation

The week after the New England area sports franchises won a championship during those nineteen years, there was always a parade. Every city in our country honors its sports heroes with a parade after they win a major championship. It's both a celebration and a thank you. It allows the city and the fans to see the stars up close that brought them so much joy in the past season.

It is one big appreciation party for everyone involved. If you talk to any professional athlete, they will tell you, that when you win the biggest game at the highest level it will make your career, and makes the thought of doing it again even sweeter. They have worked tirelessly to get to this point and this is their reward.

So where is your parade? Where is your celebration? Just because what you accomplish in"t broadcast on ESPN for the world to see doesn't mean it isn't worthy of a celebration. There are many ways to celebrate and show appreciation to ourselves and others when we achieve success. I am going to take a pause for a moment and leave the next few pages blank so you can write all the ways you would like to celebrate your wins and achievements.

Think about what different ways you would like to celebrate and who you would like to be with you when you celebrate. List the things in your life you are working towards, both big and small, that you will celebrate when they are accomplished. Enjoy this process. You have earned it.

WAYS I CELEBRATE

WHO WILL I CELEBRATE WITH

THINGS I AM WORKING ON NOW
TO CELEBRATE

How was that process for you? I am almost certain it brought a smile to your face. We all work so hard to be the best version of ourselves every day and sometimes don't feel appreciated. The biggest takeaway I want you to have from this process is we don't need outside recognition to celebrate. We can throw our parade and invite our guests to it. Celebrating all the wins big and small, and doing it often, keep us motivated to keep pushing through the hard days.

I hope you will take this exercise, implement it in your life, and share it with as many people as you can. The process of achieving results can be exhausting, so let's have some fun with it and spread this message like wildfire.

Celebrating others

Now that you have the gift of this process, let's be on the lookout for others in our lives who need help getting to the celebration phase. Like attracts like, so if you feel like celebrating was not in your weekly life, then others suffer the same fate right next to you. You won't have to look too far. You will probably see some of them tomorrow.

On the last page of this chapter, I am going to leave one more page blank for you to write on. This time, think about the people closest to you who recently had a win, big or small. Write down who they are and how you will help them celebrate their achievement. This could be the most fulfilling thing you do this week, for both you and them. I hope this process has infused some energy in you, and that we celebrate ourselves and the people who mean the most to us before we celebrate anyone else.

HOW I WILL HELP SOMEONE I KNOW CELEBRATE A RECENT WIN?

~ IX ~

FULFILLMENT OVER DOLLARS

"Success without FULFILLMENT is the ultimate failure"
-Tony Robbins

How many of you have had those days where you achieved your goal and then you asked yourself, *"Is this all there is?"* There is no worse fate than when you achieve everything, yet you still aren't fulfilled. The human mind is not going to make you happy. It's up to you to create your happiness. Unfortunately, a lot of people only strive for financial success. They think that by having more money, they will be happy.

Don't strive to only achieve financial success. Rather, strive to master the art of fulfillment. At the end of the day, the quality of your life comes down to the quality of the emotions that you consistently experience. If you can change your emotions, you can change your life.

Like it or not, much of our society is defined by achievement and the drive to go further faster and get satisfaction. The challenge with this is that our brains have yet to catch up. It's wired to constantly put us on the lookout for what's wrong, which in turn leads us to higher rates of anxiety and depression.

The key to mastering the art of fulfillment is learning to trade our expectations for appreciation. Feeling fulfilled isn't simply a matter of trading happiness for success or vice versa. There are a few habits we can learn to make part of our process in life, achieving fulfillment in our results. Remember that success with fulfillment is not an event, it is a process.

Make the decision

Decisions shape our lives. You are living the life you have today because of the decisions that you've made. The past is gone and will never return! If you aren't happy with the decisions you've made up to now, all that you can do is learn from your mistakes, move forward, and commit to making better decisions. You are in control of your destiny. The only way to shape your current life into the destiny you wish to live is by making decisions.

I believe that you can change your life by making different decisions. If you are currently on a road that isn't working for you, make a shift. The shift doesn't always have to be a major one. Oftentimes it can be small. Small shifts now have the power to alter the course of your entire life in 5-10 years. If you want fulfillment in your life, you have to make great decisions consistently. It's not the things you do on occasion that determine your success in life. Rather, it's the actions that you take daily.

Expect More Of Yourself

You can't change your life unless you are willing to raise your expectations. If you want more in life, you've got to expect more from yourself. You've got to figure out what you must do and not just what you should do. Everyone has a laundry list of things they "*should*" do. When we make a list of what you "*must*" do, it creates an urgency to take action.

History shows that when our behavior is driven by "shoulds," we lose our ability to distinguish what we really "*must*" do. As a result, we fail to take action. It's only when you fully commit to doing something, that you can take control of your life. The secret to success is learning how to balance the "shoulds" and "musts", instead of having them control your future. Ask yourself, "*What will happen by not taking action?*" Equally important, "*What are the positive benefits that will come when I take action?*"

Never Stop Improving

If you want to become fulfilled in your life, you can't stop improving in any aspect. You can't settle for the status quo if you want to have a fulfilled life. As directors of our destinies, we need to change our mindset from, "*I'm going to do what everyone else does*" to "*This is a great time to be alive because I can grow, educate, and develop my skills.*"

Work harder on yourself than anything else, because no one will do it for you. If you become more valuable, you will be able to give more, do more, and change more. This will lead to the ultimate fulfillment in your life and how you interact with others.

Giving Back

How do we give back even when it's not convenient? I believe that, if you can give, even when you don't have the money to do so, scarcity will leave your life. Giving doesn't always need to be with a dollar figure. Sometimes just giving someone your ear and listening, or giving a piece of needed advice, can give someone the will to keep moving forward and will bring you fulfillment.

Make the act of giving a must in your life. When you give, the rewards of doing so will be greater than you could ever imagine. It will give you a feeling of fulfillment no amount of money can replace. Only those who have learned the power of sincere and selfless contribution experience life's deepest joy: true fulfillment.

Who You Let Into Your Circle Matters

One of the most important decisions that you can make in your life is who you decide to let into your inner circle. So many of us have experienced pain and even failure for not protecting who we let into our inner circle. Some people can derail and poison your success. Our number one job in life is to be the goalkeeper of our inner circles. The more poison we keep out, the happier we are and the more energy we have for ourselves and others.

Have you ever had to make a phone call or meeting with someone, and you are dreading every minute of it? This person drains all of the energy you have in you and adds nothing in return. Having too many of these people in your life can single-handedly derail not only your success, but your quest for fulfillment.

When you are a part of a group of people who are living life at a high level, you automatically raise your expectations. However, if you surround yourself with people who have low standards, you will follow suit. If you want to change your life, pick and choose who you let into your inner circle.

Fame And Fortune Is Not Fulfillment

I often ask people, *"This year what do you truly want to happen to be happy?"* The answer almost always comes back with a dollar figure or material items. I get answers like...

- Make a million dollars
- Not have to work anymore
- Buy a boat
- Go on an exotic vacation
- Get into a new relationship

I have seen people acquire all of the listed items above and be truly lost or miserable. I am not saying there is no value in those things. History does show us that these things alone will not make you truly happy. People are chasing a feeling they think they will get when they acquire all of these things. Striving to get things is great, but to do so without first finding fulfillment and joy in life is a failure.

Elvis Presley, Michael Jackson, and Robin Williams, to name a few, are all people who had access to all the things mentioned in the list. From the view of the public, these people had it all. They had fame and fortune. They could fly in a private plane to an exotic island anytime they wanted. They couldn't possibly be unhappy with all the stuff they had access to.

I wish that were true, due to a lack of fulfillment they all died in the prime of their lives. Elvis Presley could have run for President of the United States if he wanted to in the 1960s and won by a landslide. He was the "*King*" of his industry. He had one of his albums in every household in America. Had a mansion that for the era was state of the art, private planes, people around him all the time, and more money than some countries. He was dead at forty-two years old.

Michael Jackson hit the scene when he was just a kid. The Jackson Five came into the world's living room when Michael was just five years old. As a ten-year-old boy, I remember watching Michael during his solo career and being in awe watching his talent and trying to mimic his moonwalk. Everyone wanted to see and be Michael Jackson.

I was also in awe as a young adult in watching Michael go from having everything to being portrayed as a criminal. It was extremely hard to watch. Michael, like Elivs, had a mansion, his own private theme park, people who loved him, and streams of income coming from all directions. You could see Michael, even with all his talents, wasn't happy with himself, and as a result, Michael Jackson died at fifty years old.

Robin Williams in my eyes was one of the funniest, most genuine people in Hollywood. I remember as a kid watching Mork and Mindy on T.V. with my family. Mrs. Doughtfire leaves me in stitches time after time. He was in 82 movies, and his stand-up was beloved by millions. I can never remember a time watching Robin Williams when he was not being funny. Even on a simple interview on a late-night talk show, he had the host and audience in stitches.

The day I heard Robin Williams was dead at sixty-three years old, it came as a surprise and not a shock, because Hollywood stars and music entertainers dying young was, unfortunately, a common story. When I heard it was suicide, I was in shock. He had it all. The money, the fame, all the stuff, and the relationships. Then he hung himself!

How senseless for someone with everything life has to offer to commit suicide after staring in 82 movies, and being loved not only by his family but by millions of people around the world. It makes you sad, then mad, then confused. We get emotional when we see these similar stories in the news media every year, that a celebrity or entertainer has died in their younger years. These are just the people we hear about that are in the public eye. Imagine all the people in the world who this happens to that we never hear about.

These three American icons put all the pieces together to have everything any of us ever want. Except for one very important piece of the puzzle. Maybe the most important piece. Fulfillment! None of the three men were fulfilled in their life. They all during parts of their career were very depressed. If you took away all the money, fame, and stuff, they were not happy with who they were and what they had to offer besides being famous. There was an emptiness inside of them no amount of money or stuff could replace.

Success without fulfillment can't be success. It is the same as when people categorize being rich with being wealthy. Being rich is not the same as being wealthy. Being rich means you have a lot of money. Being wealthy has absolutely nothing to do with money. It has everything to do with being fulfilled in the life you have created.

These tragic deaths that we have spoken about in this chapter, and all the other ones like it, hurt the most because they are avoidable. All three of these men could be alive today if they could have just shut the outside world off and focused solely on what makes them fulfilled.

If you listen to interviews and stories that come from the people closest to Elvis Presley, Michael Jackson, and Robin Williams, you will hear that they loved what they did. They enjoyed performing their craft for the world. The night after night demands from the public and their entourage is what begins to take away the fulfillment of just doing what they loved.

So many of us live every day at the demand of others, and for reasons that are not who we truly are or want to become. We get up in the morning with a sense of *"have to"*, not *"get to"*. Life is a *"get to."* Every day that passes where we are not pumped up to start the day and do the things we love to do puts us one day closer to an early grave.

~ X ~

LONELY AT THE TOP

"As we express our gratitude, we must never forget that the highest appreciation is not to utter words, but to live by them."
-John F. Kennedy

There is a *"Myth"* that gets said quite often that it is *"Lonely at the top"*. Lonely for who? Where did this saying come from? So many subconsciously come up short of what they want because most of us want to be at the top, and no one wants to be there alone. This is the definition of the phrase... *"Used to say that powerful and successful people often have few friends."*

If you achieve your goals by using the process of cheating your way to success, then yes you will be lonely. Here is my problem with this phrase, *"Lonely at the top"*. If you achieved what you set out to achieve and there is no one willing to celebrate it with you, or you did it alone, you are not at the top.

Here is a phrase or saying mentors of mine have embedded into my soul. *"No one succeeds alone."* When we practice this process, in achieving whatever we choose to achieve, then it becomes impossible to ever be *"Lonely at the top."* Success through people has been modeled for centuries and will be for centuries to come.

Take the story we have of IronMan Chris Nikic. You will read much more about him in the interview I have with him and his coach Dan Grieb. Chris decided that he would be the first person with down syndrome to ever become an IronMan. Doing it alone without the " *No one succeeds alone"* process would have taken decades longer, or even worse, never happened at all.

On November 7, 2020, after 16 hrs 46 minutes and 9 seconds, Chris was at the top. He was not lonely. He crossed that finish line and shocked the world. When he finished, who was there at the top with him? Dan, his family, other competitors, his fans, the media, and millions of people like him who now know what is possible.

You would think that Chris had completed his mission and that would be the end of his journey. This was just the beginning of a lifelong mission to lead other people with down syndrome to do what most believe is impossible. To do interview after interview, speaking engagement after speaking engagement, and IronMan after IronMan, to spread his message. Chris will reach the top of his mountain because of the people he has decided to surround himself with and will change millions of lives in the process. He is far from alone at the top.

People can be roadblocks

The phrase *"Lonely at the Top"* is just one of the many phrases and sayings we hear along the way to achieving what we want. Other phrases I have had to shake from my vocabulary are, *"Money doesn't grow on trees", "The rich get richer," "To make money you have to spend money,"* and *"Don't forget where you came from."*

All of these phrases are part of a bigger belief system that makes people not want to begin the process of getting what they want. I am totally fine if there are people out there that believe in these phrases. I only ask that you keep it to yourself and not poison the rest of us with that limited thinking.

A few years ago my wife and I started to branch out and build our real estate investment portfolio. We had acquired a lot of knowledge over the years being in the real estate business and had attended many seminars on how to follow the correct process to start building a rental portfolio. We found a partner who we met during some of these seminars and started to acquire some short-term rentals with him in Daytona Beach, Florida. We have hit our fair share of challenges and bumps in the road along the way and have learned some valuable lessons we did not anticipate.

The most disturbing unforeseen challenge we faced had nothing to do with the real estate we were buying. It had to do with some people in our inner circle who started with these phrases of limiting beliefs. I remember one in particular who said, *"Why would you ever want to be a landlord."* Another said, *"Are you forgetting where you came from?"*

Seriously? We invested in a few properties that we researched and got educated on using a process we had studied for three years, and I forgot where we came from? I immediately knew that if we were to achieve the goal of building this portfolio that we needed to find success through others who had the same mindset as us.

Having someone who you love and respect not see happiness in what you have achieved or are achieving, and can only see the negative, can completely screw with your mind and confidence. Yes, it can even make you feel lonely in some situations. This is the point where decisions need to be made on who you let into your circle.

How We Guarantee It Won't Be Lonely At The Top

There will be many people in your life who will have their fingerprints all over your success. Some will be family, some friends, some colleagues. Whomever it is will join you in celebration at the top, as long as you treat them with honor and respect along the way. When you achieve your goals and look around, you will see people from past and present who helped you get to the top of your mountain.

What is funny about our journey is that someone could show you something or give you mentorship in one year, and then years or even decades later, that mentorship will push you over the last hurdle of the mountain. No one gets to the top of their mountain without help, and how we treat the people who helped us get there will define us.

Top executives in corporate America have the biggest challenges in the *"Lonely at the top"* syndrome. Working their way up through the company over several years. Along the way, they are now the boss of the same people who were colleagues of just a few months or years before.

That situation can be so challenging for someone on both sides of it. It can be challenging for the executive who has to go from being someone's colleague and now having to lead them every day. It is the trust and respect that was built during the time of being colleagues that will inevitably be the factor that makes the relationship work.

Had the executive not carried themselves with integrity, honor, and respect for others, this new relationship structure could not work. Because the executive built such trusting relationships with colleagues, the people that he or she now leads are happy for their success.

No one ever has to be *"lonely at the top."* The next time you achieve something you are proud of, look around. If the people you would like to be there with you to celebrate are not there, ask yourself why. Is it because you didn't keep them in your good graces? We have a choice moving forward on how we approach the top of the mountain. Remember, the person working alongside you today could be the key to your success tomorrow.

~ XI ~

I MADE IT, NOW WHAT?

"Creativity is intelligence having fun."
- **Albert Einstein**

Hitting your goal or dream can be the most rewarding, and the scariest thing at the same time. You have worked day after day, month after month, and often year after year, to achieve your goal or dream. The road you took to get there was completely different than you originally thought, and yet here you are. The process you have followed has been successful. *"Now what?"*

This question has haunted so many people over the years and will haunt many more to come. The *"Now what"* question comes from many places. First, it comes from those of us who have struggled hard to achieve this level of success, and have always had something stand or get in our way. So the question *"Now what?"* refers to the saying, *"Waiting for the other shoe to drop."* In other words, what is going to happen now to take it all away?

We have all had this happen to us. The process to overcome it and move to the next step in your journey is explained in this section in detail. It is called the rinse and repeat process. The rinse and repeat process in a short description is to look at the habits and rituals that have aided in you achieving your goal or dream and don't stop. Continue to be that person.

The other reason we ask ourselves the *"Now what?"* question, is we are chasing the idea that this goal or dream will give us a certain feeling that we want or think we need. Then when the goal or dream is achieved, the feeling we thought we would have doesn't show up. Or worse, we assign so many rules around the goal or dream, we make it unobtainable.

For example, have you ever heard someone state a goal just to state a goal? A common one is, *"I want to make a billion dollars."* I ask, *"For what?" "What about that billion dollars is so important to you?"* Most of the time the person can not answer that question. After doing some digging, I find out they think making a billion dollars will mean they will never have to work again and they can be financially free.

Here is the reality. They can achieve that goal with a heck of a lot less than a billion dollars. When we go through the process of actually breaking down how much they would need to be financially free and not have to work again we find the dollar amount is a few million dollars in assets returning them a 5% return yearly to live the lifestyle they want.

We do not have to be math or financial wizards to figure that a few million is a lot less than a billion. Let's say no one ever went through this process with them. They continue to go around thinking they need a billion dollars and have no plan on how to get there. What is their likely outcome? The likely outcome is an absolute failure and suffering. They have made their goal or dream unreachable. We need to be sure that when we make a goal or strive for a dream, we know why the outcome is important.

The final piece to the whole *"Now what?"* scenario, is getting where we are going and being lonely. We get where we want to go but we bring no one along to enjoy it with. Let's say you sell the business you have spent decades building, and financially you are set for life. What will fill the void of time that was previously occupied by the business? Even more important than that, what will fill the void of you feeling needed or connections with the people you had from that business?

Not having a plan in place to go and start the next thing, even if it's a small thing, can lead to massive anxiety, loneliness, and depression. Let's step away from the business talk for a moment and give an example of this in everyday life. Let's take the all-American family. Mom and Dad get married and buy a home. They want to start a family and have two children. For the next eighteen to twenty years or more, the parents spend all their focus and energy on making sure they give their children more than they had to set them up for a successful life.

The children graduate school and begin their own lives. Mom and Dad have not discussed or thought about what they may do next. A few years go by, or even less time in some cases, and Mom and Dad start to drift apart and begin living separate lives. They say they have grown apart and are not the same people as they were when they got married.

So much of this could have been avoided by having a vision for what they may like to have, do, or experience together in their later years. When we are in the moment and everything moves so fast, as it always does, we need a process to slow us down and cause us to examine what we may like to do

Rinse and repeat
"Success is not final, failure is not fatal: it is the courage to continue that counts."
-Winston Churchill

As a business coach and a business owner who has had his hands in different cookie jars, I can say from what I have seen and experienced that we make having success in the next venture entirely too difficult for ourselves.

I remember when I transitioned from selling real estate full time, to being a coach full time. The first six months were a brutal reality check. I was failing miserably at achieving success in signing clients and could not get over the hump. I was second-guessing my decision to make this a full-time career. I kept asking myself the same question, *"What do I have to do to show the value?"*

I asked this question out loud to the right person at the right time. He was a fellow coach who had a little more time than me in generating his client base. After I asked him this question, he made a statement that will live in my mind until the day I die. He said, *"Well Zip, you just came from a career where you had to go and find your clients, show them the value in working with you, and close the business. What did you do every day that made you successful in that career?"*

That was so simple. It was so simple I felt like a fraud in business to not have thought of it myself. Take the habits, rituals, and supportive people I had around me to create that success, and apply them to this opportunity. That is exactly what I did, and then the rinse and repeat process was born. We have all had a time when we have felt absolutely in the zone and unstoppable. We need to channel the person we became to achieve success. We need to call on them every time we are in a situation when we need them. We don't recreate a new person every time we start something new. We bring back the person who gets it done.

It may not always be the same venture or goal we are chasing. Always it is the same process. Let's use legendary NFL quarterback Tom Brady for example. For twenty seasons with the New England Patriots, he led the team to nine Super Bowls and won six of them. In 2020, he decided to end his time with New England and change colors to the Tampa Bay Buccaneers.

Many thought this would be a career killer. The Tampa Bay Buccaneers had very little history of success. They had only one Super Bowl victory in their entire franchise history. Nevertheless, Brady packed up his family and said goodbye to his twenty-year home in New England, and moved to Tampa.

In the first few weeks, Brady and the Bucs were nothing more than an average team. In fact, in the first game of the season, Drew Brees and the New Orleans Saints dismantled Tom Brady and the Buccaneers 34 - 23. How poorly the Bucs played did not show in the score, as the game was mostly one-sided.

As you could imagine the media went into a frenzy. Everyone thought Tom Brady had just made the worst possible career move he could have ever imagined. Or did he? After that, the Bucs won the next 6 out of 7 games. Most of the games they won convincingly. He even recruited and brought out of retirement his old pal and go-to tight end, Rob Gronkowski.

So halfway through the season, Brady started showing signs that the *"Rinse and Repeat"* process works. He admitted that the pre-season and first few games were rough. They had to work to get all these players who individually had amazing talent, to work as a team. As the weeks went on, Brady went back to the things that had made him successful in New England and apply them to his new team. Gronkowski was not the only former Patriot that Brady brought to the Bucs. Late in the season, he knew to win the big game he needed one more threat to throw the ball to. He made a phone call and the Bucs acquired former Patriot Antonio Brown.

This was as controversial a move as any team could have made. Antonio Brown was a long-time leading receiver for the Pittsburgh Steelers. In 2019, he decided he would move his career elsewhere and joined the Oakland Raiders. From day one, Brown could not get this relationship to work. There were countless times when Brown and the Raiders would make media headlines for things not related to football. Some of them were Antionio Brown's doing.

After several agonizing weeks, and Antonio Brown not taking one second of field time in a regular-season game, he was let go by the Raiders. A few games into the 2019 season, he was signed by the New England Patriots. Tom Brady was over the moon excited to add a threat like Antonio Brown to his offense. They played a game in Miami and the two future Hall of Famers lit up the Miami Dolphins in front of their home crowd.

Later that week, Antonio Brown was accused of sexual misconduct and was going to be formally charged. The Patriots, after only one game together, released Brown from the Patriots. Later that year Brown was acquitted of the charges. So you can see why everyone was so surprised that Brady would be so quick to want to bring Brown to his new team.

Now we will never really know what the conversions with Gronkowski and Brown looked like that would convince both of them to go on this crusade with Brady, but I imagine it was something like this. "Gronk, I am going to the Super Bowl this year, Do you want to come?" and for Brown, " Antionio, I enjoyed the time we spent in New England even though it was short. I am going to the Super Bowl this year. Do you want to come?"

Again, I will probably never get the exclusive interview with these players to find out the real words used, but I would guess that was the conversation. Not only did these two tremendous players come and join the mission by Brady's side, but they also went on to play in that year's Super Bowl against the defending Super Bowl Champion, Kansas City Chiefs.

Patrick Mahomes and the Chiefs had recently taken the crown from the former King's of the AFC, Tom Brady, and the New England Patriots. This matchup could not have been a better storyline for NFL fans or the media. To boot, for the first time in Super Bowl history, a team would get to play a Super Bowl in their home stadium.

So In Super Bowl LV, Tom Brady takes back his crown as King of the NFL, as the Bucs beat the Chiefs 31-9. There is a lot to talk about in this score, and this is not a book about football, but the stats speak for themselves. Brady followed the process by using habits and rituals that made him successful in the past. By acquiring Gronkowski and Brown, he set himself up with people who helped with his past success.

During that Super Bowl, Gronkowski scored two Touchdowns and Brown scored one. Making up 21 of the 31 points scored in the game by the Bucs. This is an example of how the *"Rinse and Repeat"* process worked for football. It doesn't only define that one player in their quest for greatness, but the whole team. It also proves that when we want to venture out and work toward something new, we don't have to reinvent who we are. We just bring out the person who has always gotten the job done, and continue to be them.

Putting it all together

Over the past 11 Chapters, we have gone over a broad variety of processes to improve your overall quality of life, both at home and at work. The intention was for you to identify with the three amazing individuals who were interviewed, as well as my experiences and the stories of others. Identifying helps us see things as possible vs just a dream. In the final chapter, you will read the three interviews and pull even more tools that you can integrate into your daily life.

Putting it all together is the key that unlocks your success using the tools in this book. Not everything in the book will resonate with you and that's ok. When something does, make a note and find a way to take action. It is the only way to make an everlasting change.

I hope you enjoyed reading this as much as I enjoyed writing it. Helping other people move forward is something we all get to do at one point in life, and my wish is this will help you, and in turn, you will use it to help others.

Finally, I challenge you to spread this message. If this book moved you, then send five copies to people who can benefit from everything I have shared here. The mission is to help as many people as possible achieve an extraordinary life.

~ XII ~

THE INTERVIEWS

"People say there are two kinds of learning: experience, which is gained from your own mistakes, and wisdom, which is learned from the mistakes of others."
- John C. Maxwell

The following interviews may be the most valuable pieces of this book. It is an opportunity to see how real-life people take all the processes we have talked about and generate huge results. The three stories are very different, and yet when you take away the individual details, they are very much the same. They achieved success by being purposeful about a process.

The first interview is a real-life Cinderella story. It is the story of how Chris Nikic became the first person with Down syndrome to complete the IronMan race. We go through his journey of finding the right coach and handler to help him accomplish this mission. Chris and his coach Dan Grieb walk us through how they met, how they accomplished the Iron Man, and what's next in their journey.

CHRIS NIKIC INTERVIEW

F: Hi, Chris.

C: Hey.

F: How are you doing? Good to meet you.

F: Here with Dan Grieb, Chris Nikic

F: We're putting a book together called *The Process* – the process of being able to accomplish anything you want to by just following a process. I would love to just hear how you guys met and how this partnership came together.

C: I was born, and I had this genetic disorder, that's called Down syndrome. For the next 18 years, I've been at home, playing lots of fear games, and I got fed up with people who were telling me that I can't do anything. I"d tell them; you need to stop listening to experts.

D: I met Chirs at the Special Olympics. Chris was doing a sprint triathlon.

D: Chris was looking for someone that can help him do the further distance called an Olympic. He did a sprint triathlon, which is about a 10-mile race, and now he was wanting to do a 30-mile race. And he was looking for someone to help him and at the same time,

I had gone through this big weight loss journey, where I'd lost 100 pounds. I had set this goal to do 10 Ironman competitions in two years. I had completed my 10th Ironman, and I was getting ready to retire. At that point, I decided that it was about time for me to retire, focus on other things, and I wanted to express my gratitude to God for getting back my health in my 40s and I figured what's the best way to do that, other than to help someone else become an Ironman.

As you know, success is not about what you do, it's about who you become. And for me to become an Ironman, it required me to get very diligent about what I ate, learn how to wake up on time, and follow the systems and processes that an Ironman has to follow, it involves a lot of individual training. It's an individual sport, requires a lot of discipline when it comes to diet, nutrition, exercise, rehab, and sleep.

I went on a quest to find someone that I could help become an Ironman. At that time, the only person that could be an Ironman or that needed your help was either a blind person, or an incapacitated person, someone who couldn't swim, bike, or run by themselves. I was having an extremely difficult time finding someone.

I couldn't find anyone. I was thinking, you know, maybe, God doesn't want me to do this. Then one day, Chris and his dad showed up in one of our triathlon meetings, looking for a very intense guy, that had a big heart and could step away from his career and his training for six months to a year to help Chris do more training, and that's how it all began.

F: Chris, before you met Dan, what's the furthest you had ever gone running or bicycle?

C: 10 miles.

F: 10 miles?

F: 10 miles and then an Ironman is how many miles?

C: 112

F: Wow. One of the most inspiring parts about this whole journey from what I've seen so far is this 1% better mentality. I love 1% better. Can you guys explain the 1% better process?

C: I was better today than I was yesterday.

D: When Chris started, he started with one push-up, one sit-up, and one squat.

C: And then I went up to 200 of everything.

D: Before Ironman, he went all the way up to 200 push-ups, sit-ups, and squats.

D: Before we get to Hawaii, he and I are going to do 500 push-ups, sit-ups, and squats together in one sitting. We break them up into pieces.

F: What are the rules to get in 1% Better?

C: Smile

D: Well, first off, we do everything with a smile because nobody likes a what?

C: A Grouchy person.

F: Okay. Number two is what?

C: No crying.

F: And what's number three?

C: No excuses

D: So, the idea behind 1% better is simply this: Chris doesn't think like you and I do. He doesn't operate like you and I do. He does have an intellectual disability called Down syndrome. Basically, for you and I, this is our brain – we have five different lanes of traffic and traffic can fly freely down all those lanes. Well, Chris only has two lanes of traffic. All five lanes have to merge into those two lanes.

What we've noticed is Chris has a disability that is also his superhero advantage as well. Now as we teach Chris things, we recognize the fact that we have to teach him through repetition. The good news about Chris is, he loves repetition.

C: Yeah.

D: So, he likes to eat at the same places all the time. You liked to eat at IHOP and McDonald's, right?

C: Yes. And the Waffle House.

D: Okay. So those are the three places he likes to eat, and that's where he goes all the time. Well, what we recognize also is, Chris isn't operating from ego. You and I, want to prove to the world that we can do something. We want to prove that we can accomplish something, and Chris just wants to be included.

He'll explain what inclusion means later. We had to figure out a strategy to teach him how to learn skills at a level that makes sense to him. That's what 1% better is. The concept is that there's a compounding effect of, if I go from one push-up to two push-ups or from two push-ups to three, I can go from three to four. So, one of the things we don't want to do is, we do not want to put Chris in a lot of pain, because if he recognizes that working out with Dan is painful, he's not going to work out with me anymore.

Most people like me, go crazy trying to accomplish something, and then we get injured, we get burned out and we say, the hell with that, I don't want to do that anymore. With Chris, we have to teach him so slowly because of his intellectual capacity. Also, we don't want him to experience a lot of pain. His dad came up with the methodology of 1% better and I just adopted it.

It's easier for Chris to do 101 push-ups, and then a couple of days later, do 103 push-ups as it is for him to go from one pushup to two push-ups. For you and me, our growth trajectory looks like this. We start at the bottom, go up to here then we level off. Well, with Chris, what his growth trajectory looks like is a geometric progression. He's spending months and months, building this small undercurrent of success, this small foundation.

He's going from a 13-minute mile to a 13-minute mile to a 13-minute mile to a 12.59, 12.59, 12.59, and it goes on and on 12.58. I mean, it seems so small, the growth in terms of its incremental piece that it almost feels like he's not growing at all. And then all of a sudden, when everyone else starts slowing down or backsliding, he starts catching up and overtaking them. A perfect example of that is when Chris started his first sprint. What place did you come in when you did your first sprint triathlon?

C: Last.

D: You came in last?

C: Yeah.

D: And how far behind the last person were you? Do you remember?

C: 1 hour behind

D: He was almost an hour behind. Okay. Then those athletes started taking time off and they stopped training with COVID. Well, Chris kept training. Next race, he still came in last. But he came in 20 minutes later than the last one. So, it was an hour the first time now it's 20 minutes. Then before we know it, now he's completing a 70.3 distance race, and none of them can do that.

For him, he just slowly grew. And then before we know it, he had this undercurrent that can make it work. That's what getting 1% better is about. It's a compounding effect that is so small that it doesn't bring pain. It doesn't give you burnout. It gives you a habit that you can build on day after day. And remember, the human brain enjoys winning.

F: Do you like to win Chris?

C: Yeah.

D: If you and I played basketball, who would win right now?

C: I will.

D: You'd win?

C: Yeah.

D: What if we played in the pool? Would you win then too?

C: I will.

D: Who's going to win in Hawaii?

C: I will.

D: I'm going to win.

C: I will.

D: See, he's so competitive. Just because he has Down syndrome doesn't mean he doesn't like to win. Well, if he can do one and then two, that's a win for him, two to three is a win for him. So, we give him these small wins. His brain is different than yours and mine. When he wins he feels good about it. We want to give him the ability to keep feeling good about it. And that's what we do. That's 1% better.

F: This 1% process, how many years has this been going on?

D: For him, he's been training for about two and a half years. To go from the couch to an Ironman took him about two years, and he was overweight.

F: Talk to me about inclusion. What about inclusion? What does that mean?

C: Kids with Down syndrome need to realize that they can live a life of inclusion, they can be independent, they can live on their own, have their own house, have a car, and marry.

D: And for people like Chris, he has a support structure through high school because he's got other kids in class with him that are like him. Once they leave the high school, then they call that falling off the cliff. There are no services, there's no inclusion for them. For Chris and his family, what they wanted to do was get him involved in an activity where he could learn lifelong habits of health. Then he could find a community around him. What's happened now, is he has a team now. What's the name of the team that you're on? You're on a bunch of teams. What's the one here in Florida you're on?

C: Triathlon Club.

D: He's on the Orlando Triathlon Club. He has a community that supports him, and he has the Triathlon Club. How many families do you have right now? Your family, the Nikics', and who else do you have a family with?

C: You.

D: So, you're part of who else's family?

C: Uncle Dan's family.

D: And what do you call my wife Mindy?

C: Aunt.

D: Aunt Mindy?

C: Yeah.

D: And what do you call my kids, Riley and Drew?

C: Brothers.

D: He's got two new brothers and an aunt and an uncle. None of us knew this, but people with Down syndrome would die young, they would die in their 40s, they wouldn't make it. But now, they're living longer and longer because we're understanding Down syndrome. We're understanding how to keep them active and moving.

What's happening is that folks with Down syndrome are now outliving their parents. So, parents of children with Down syndrome have now got this new worry of what's going to happen to our child when we pass away? And for the Nikics', they were praying for someone younger than them to take care of Chris when they passed away. They say I'm an answer to their prayers and of course Mindy, my wife.

F: Awesome. Along this process, you did something that's probably one of the most physically demanding things a human person can do. During that race, was there any point where you thought you wouldn't finish?

D: Let's start here, what about the swim? How did you feel in the swim? So, remember what you told me? You said that the waves were hitting you in the mouth, and what did I tell you to do when the waves started getting choppy and scaring you? Take a what?

C: Take a deep breath, focus, and keep going

D: Keep going, right? And several times the waves got choppy, right? And where do they hit you?

C: In the mouth.

D: Well, it made it tough for you to do what?

C: Breathe.

D: It made it tough for you to breathe. And then what did you say to yourself?

C: Keep fighting.

D: Just keep fighting. So, in the water, we had some challenges.

F: Right off the bat.

D: Right out of the gate, and then I had a goggle malfunction. He and I did practice swimming there on the course, but we didn't get a chance to discuss the logistics with who was going to be in the water with us. We didn't know how that was going to work. This was the first Ironman all year that has not been canceled. Every Ironman had been canceled all year. This is the only one that was held in 2020 after COVID came to the United States. They had a sold-out race; they ran a 70.3 and a half Ironman the same day.

We had two groups of athletes, half and full, happening on the same day. Then on top of it, you have Chris, who's got millions of views online, newspaper reporters, television cameras, and worldwide coverage of us doing this race. Well, we didn't talk logistics.

The next issue we ran into was, we had photographers in front of us in a kayak. Then we had rescue crews to our right because the last thing they want is the first person with Down syndrome to drown during the Ironman. Rescue people to my right, crew to my front, photographers to my front, and a guided boat. Nobody told me I would have that.

When we swim, my job is to keep him on pace and keep Chris going in the right direction. We have these different buoys that we have to go around. There was a photographer in front of me and a guided boat in front of me at different times. What they did is they made it so I couldn't see the buoys. So, we never knew whether we were swimming in the right direction. That was our first big challenge.

C: Yes.

D: Then the next thing is we were off on the bike. We got started on the bike. Again, Chris has this issue with processing things. So anytime an event occurs that he's not used to, processing slows down. When processing slows down, that means muscles move slower, everything moves slower, his brain moves slower, his body moves slower. His everything goes a little bit slower.

One of the things that I do for Chris is I help him on his bike, I push him, and he goes. Then I ride and catch up with him. Then I ride right next to him and I yell commands to him. He has hearing aids in but he doesn't wear hearing aids during the race so I have to talk very loud. Every 30 to 40 minutes depending on how hot it is, I have to ride ahead of him again, get him to stop, catch him because he doesn't have good balance, get him off of his bike, lay his bike down, and then give him the proper amount of nutrition and hydration. Very quickly get him back on his bike and have him ride again. Well, what happened when we got off the bike at mile 20?

C: I stepped into a red ant pile.

F: You stepped into a red ant pile?
Oh, man!

C: Then they bit me.

D: They bit you where?

C: Everywhere!

D: I noticed that I had got bitten by an ant, I didn't realize that he was physically standing in an ant pile. I see him standing in an ant pile. Then I see he was in the moment. So, when he was in the moment, he didn't recognize he had ants up his legs into his groin area. I had to take all of our available water and wash him down and clean him up. I had to take his socks off, get another athlete to give me their socks, put socks on him, and go.

At the same time, I'm freaking out, but I can't let him know that I'm freaking out because I don't know if he's allergic to ant bites. We had prepared for everything. We prepared for, if he crashes, to take him to this hospital. What did he eat the day before? What does he eat now? What is the allergic to, food-wise?

If I need to feed him anything I know how to. How to deal with vision problems, hearing problems. Anything that could happen, we talked about it all. We did not talk about, what if he stands in an ant pile. And so, I didn't know if maybe he had an allergic reaction to red ants. I had a radio on me so I could radio another guide. Then that guide had a cell phone and she stopped and called his dad and said, Hey, Chris has entered a red ant pile.

That was our first major challenge on the bike. Then, about 10 miles later, Chris is complaining that his eyes are hurting him. So, I'm like, "oh, great. He's reacting to all these ant bites, and now his eyes are hurting him." I went through all this checklist. He wears prescription sunglasses, so I'm thinking maybe the sun's too bright. I'm just thinking through all of it. I'm washing his eyes out, but he keeps complaining about it.

So now, I figured out that what was getting in his eyes was sunblock. So, I got the sunblock out of his eye and got him going again. But now he's had ant bites and sunblock in his eye, and he needs to see his dad. He recharges with hugs and connections. I can do about 95% of any of his issues, but Dad gets him over the hump if there's a hump.

Now understand, as soon as his eyes started hurting, his speed goes from 17 – 18 miles an hour to 11 miles an hour. We are not making it at that pace. He's already forgotten about the ant bites. That's where Chris has a disability that's also a superpower. Chris is in the moment. As soon as the ant bites were over, and I say, "*Chris, we got to move on*", and we're going again, a minute or two later, he's forgotten about the ant bites. I mean, they might be painful, but he's not thinking about the ant bite stuff as you and I would think about it.

C: We saw my dad, he looked at my ant bites, and then he said you have to ride.

D: Then you got started, and you started going down the hill. You started going way too fast. What happened?

C: I crashed.

F: He crashed his bike in front of his dad, going downhill. How fast were you going when you crashed? Do you remember?

C: 21 Mile per hour

D: So, he crashed. He was going too fast. He got out of control. He hit a bump, as I was telling him to slow down because we had just launched him off again. I needed to catch up to him. I caught up to him. He was going too fast and he crashed. We crashed his bike in front of his dad.

C: Yes

D: Then we got on the run and what happened at mile 10. You hit the what?

C: The wall.

D: Hit the wall. What is the wall? When your body starts to what?

C: To hurt. My legs, and stomach

D: So, he hit the wall, which is very normal. Most athletes hit the wall but they normally hit the wall at mile 20 – he hit the wall at mile 10. So here we are at mile 10 and he's struggling. We had to call his dad. His dad came and met us at mile 13. And what did your dad say to you at mile 13?

C: He said, *"Chris who's going to win today, your fake pain or your dreams?"*
I said *"My Dreams!"*
So, my number one dream is to have a house.

C: My number two, is to have a car.

C: My number three is to get married

D: So those are his dreams. See, what people misunderstand about Chris is that they think that his dream was to be an Ironman. Your dreams are not to be an Ironman, are they?

C: No. My dreams are to have my own house, have my car, and then marry a smoking hot blonde.

D: His goal was not to be an Ironman, the goal was for him to live independently, own his own house, and have his car. He knew that Ironman was a vehicle for him to go become a professional speaker, so he can get a car, get a house, and do that. A lot of people are unaware of their dreams. You ask him, what are your dreams? He'll tell you. Chris, how badly do you want a wife?

C: Right now.

D: Right now?

C: Right now.

D: And tell him, you're not what?

C: Waiting.

D: You're not waiting any longer?

C: No.

D: He'll call me and say, Uncle Dan, I need you to get me a wife right now. I'm not waiting any longer, right?

C: Yeah.

F: He's on the right path. That's for sure.

D: He tells his dad that too. He's aware of his dreams. I think that a lot of people forget that.

F: Yes.

D: They think that the big goal is the dream. The big goal is not the dream, the big goal is just the opportunity to go into the dream.

F: Yes. So, on the day of that race, I was in Jamaica, Montego Bay with my wife. I watched the end of that race on Facebook Live. With two miles left; you guys had a moment where you got ready for the last two miles of that race. What were you thinking? You can hear the crowds; you can see they're getting bigger. Everything's about to happen – everything you guys worked for these past couple of years. What was going through your mind?

D: Well, Chris, why don't you answer that. When it was the last two miles and we were getting close to the finish line, what were you thinking?

C: I was thinking I was in the moment.

C: I was getting the wife, the house, and the car.

D: He saw his dreams, he knew that the finish line was the beginning of his chance. For me, when we had two miles left, I knew we had 54 minutes left to make it. I knew that we could walk it in at that point, we could just literally walk it in. That was the first time I permitted myself to enjoy the race. Up until then, I was the guide, I was the muscle, I was the mule helping him get across.

This was not about me, it was about him. My job was to facilitate him, accomplishing his goal. At that point, I looked up and I said, *"Okay, I'm going to enjoy this."* I said to Chris, *"Listen, we're two miles out. We can take it easy if we want to."* He was not going to – we're going to run it in harder than we've run the last 24 miles. We were running the last two miles fast.

What I wanted for Chris is, I want him to be an example for other people with Down syndrome and intellectual disabilities. I wanted him to make it tougher for the ones that come behind him. I don't want the next person with Down syndrome to just finish an Ironman. They should finish it as Chris finished it.

The astounding part is before you know it Down syndrome athletes are just competing as age groupers do. It won't be a spectacle, like, *"Oh my gosh. Look, the Down syndrome kid completed an Ironman."* People will say, that Down syndrome people like competing at a super high level. So, he and I ran it in and I made this deal with him. He was hurting. But Chris likes to make deals, don't you?

C: Yeah.

D: And what else? What do you love about people? What do you like to do with people?

C: Hug them.

D: He loves to hug people. So, I say, *"Chris, I'll tell you what, if you give me the next two miles at your personal best, I'll let you hug all of your friends when we get back."* What did we do, as soon as we saw people that were wearing the 1% shirt?

C: Hug them.

D: We stopped and we hugged them, right? Then we stopped and we hug our team that was there. We hugged his friends. Who was there? Abigail and Anna Marie and their parents, both have Down syndrome, we hugged them. And then we hugged our coach, Hector. We got to hug all of the friends along the way and he got to enjoy the moment.

A lot of people when they do an Ironman when you get to the actual end of the finisher shoot and you enter the carpet area, they sprint and they want to finish strong. I've never taught Chris that and I never teach any of my athletes that. I say, listen, you completing an Ironman 15 seconds early is not going to make a big difference. When you enter that shoot, you take a moment. You take that moment of being in the lights, you allow that crowd to infect you and you just enjoy that. So, Chris loves to sprint at the end. I held him back and said no sprinting, you're going to enjoy this moment.

F: That's awesome.

D: And what am I exactly saying as we were finishing?

C: Ironman!!!

F: I remember when you finished your first one, Dan. I'd see you a lot, almost every day when you finish your first Ironman. What an accomplishment that was for you. Where does this one rank?

D: When you're a young man, especially with the life I lived, you pray that God would somehow find a way to let you be valuable in this world. I used to think my whole life that I would change the world by changing my family tree. That was not God's intention. God gave me something better. I changed someone else's world. That's more important.

Not only did we change it for Chris, but we also changed it for every other person with Down syndrome. People with Down syndrome are told that they will not amount to much. Their parents are told, you have a child with Down syndrome, and they give them the option of having an abortion and terminating the pregnancy.

When you don't, the doctors and experts say, *"Well, your child is probably not going to amount to much, you're going to get a lifetime of servanthood ahead of you."* From now on for the rest of humanity, they'll say, *"What about Chris Nikic? He's an Ironman."* I felt the weight of the Down syndrome world on my back as we were finishing that race.

I could feel their relief, that collectively as a population, they now know that they can amount to anything. Chris is an example of that. You always say I want to go viral, or I hope my story goes viral, my book goes viral. Until you've gone viral, you have no idea what going viral is. Chris gets the majority of it. You go to bed one day, you wake up, and Chris has 20,000 followers on Instagram. You wake up the next morning he has 60,000 followers.

We went to bed late that night. We were up at four o'clock and we went to bed at one o'clock in the morning. I woke up that next morning, I had over a hundred private messages from people all around the world saying, *"Thank you so much for what you did with Chris, and thank you for what you did for my kid."*

F: Wow!

D: So where does it rank? I have to say right behind having my children and getting married. A close third would be this. The whole process of meeting Chris, training Chris, living life with Chris, and then becoming an Ironman with Chris.

F: That's pretty awesome. You're an Ironman now, Chris. You're an Ironman.

C: Yeah.

F: To the whole world, if you said, *"I'm an Ironman and I'm done"*, it would have said, *"He completed the Ironman and he can be done."* But you're not done. You've got another race coming up, don't you?

C: Yeah.

F: Where are you guys going?

C: We're going to Kona World Championship, the world's biggest Ironman that has ever been done.

F: That's pretty amazing. I don't know if they have red ants in Kona. I don't think they do.

D: No, I don't think they do either.

F: So that will be helpful.

D: What is funny is that, why do I have to get off this call? What do you think is the reason why I have to get off this call early right now?

F: You got to go work out?

D: He doesn't have to work out as hard as I do. If he fails, because of him, that's not a problem. If we fail because of me, that is a problem. So, I work out three times a day, every day until October. Every day, seven days a week, I'm working out three times a day. I've already done a strength workout today. I'll do another strength workout today and I'll bike tonight.

I have to get stronger than I've ever been before. The conditions being so much more difficult, he'll need more of my help in this next race. It's the greatest honor I ever had in my whole life. So,

I'll leave you with this. The process of building a relationship with Chris was, introduction as a person, becoming his coach, earning the right to be his guide, and now I'm his uncle. It started with me doing a race with Chris, and now it's me doing the rest of my life with Chris. That's the real benefit and gift to this. The same is true with you, right Chirs?

C: Yes it is.

D: You're going to be with me the rest of my life?

C: Yeah.

F: Hey guys, I've enjoyed this.
       Thanks, guys. I appreciate it.

DAVID BERLANT INTERVIEW

My interview with David Berlant was a treat for me. Like so many others living in Central Florida, I have had the privilege of watching his journey firsthand over the past several years. He has gone from someone who had a vision, to someone living that vision every day. Everyone will learn from this story. Then if you are young, with high goals, and are not sure how to make it happen, pay extra close attention.

F: Can you introduce yourself and just kind of start from the beginning on like, your journey as an early entrepreneur?

D: Yeah. Well, I'm David Berlant, 27 years old. I started real estate when I was 19. However, if you want to talk about entrepreneurship, it goes way back to middle school. I remember my parents would go to Costco and we would buy candy and gum at wholesale prices. I remember buying candy like Skittles, and I would take it to school, and my cost per unit was $1, I would sell it for two bucks. Selling candy and gum to my friends and my teachers was just an early sign of entrepreneurship.

Then in high school, I decided to take business classes called BPA. Business Professionals of America endorsed entrepreneurship early in life. There was an actual competition every year, and it was an entrepreneurship competition.

There were all these different categories that you can apply for. I remember, one of the ones I did was having to build my own business. You had to create a business plan and then go into a competitive tournament against other schools and students. You would pitch the idea of this business to get a loan from the bank. I won, I got first place and my company was J and D Landscaping. I'm not a landscaper, but I pitched the whole process of landscaping and what I would do with a $100,000 investment.

F: It was like Shark Tank before Shark Tank.

D: Exactly. It's very funny just thinking back on it, and how this was all building from that. Now more than ever, I'm grateful that I did that. Being a top producer in my area, for me, it's really helpful to know that this isn't just something I came up with overnight. The people I talked to, especially on our team, I say, "Listen, look at me, although I have years of real estate experience, I've been developing this entrepreneurship my whole life. Although you may not be ready to make 100 or 200 or $500,000 this year, you can build to that, you just have to start now.

F: That's great advice. How many full-time years is this for you now in real estate?

D: Full-time years? It would be five years. When I joined Keller Williams in 2015, that was when I was working full time. Before that, in 2013 is when I got my license. I was working with my dad but I was also 19 and wasn't spending enough time in business. I was just having fun as a college-age kid.

F: What's been the process in the past five to six years for you to get from where you started in 2015 to where you are now? What's that process look like?

D: Yeah, I think it's all about having the right coach and having the right people to help inspire you. You know Dan Grieb well, he was a big inspiration for everything that I learned to get me into production.

He focuses on not just helping you sell real estate, but in all aspects of your life. And if you don't commit to getting better in all areas of your life, there will be gaps. I remember early on, he said, *"David, you're making some money and you're doing good and all but you're not in that greatest shape. You need to go work out."* Me being twenty-one at the time, I said, *"Okay, whatever, let's go do it."*

So, I went and started working out. I was waking up earlier than I had ever woken up in my life. I did that every day, going to the gym, and then running five K's and 10 K's, and then eventually, I ran a half marathon. Those things get your body right. I had a good business but I didn't have great health, I didn't have a great relationship with my family, I didn't have a girlfriend. Once we started filling in the blanks, that's when everything blew up.

Shortly after that, when I got into shape, Dan said, *"David, you're in good shape, you're making more money than you ever made in your entire life. When was the last date that you went on?"* I said, *"Never."* I didn't go on dates. I just was too busy working and getting into shape. He said, *"David if you do not go on a date, I will fire you from the team."* In my head, I didn't think he would fire me. However, I remember a couple of weeks went by and he asked me how it went. I said, *"I didn't go on any dates."* He said, *"David, you have until this week or else you are gone."* Sure enough, that week I went on a dating app and found a date.

We ended up dating for three months, and it was a really good experience. It led me up to where I am today, where I'm engaged to a beautiful Venezuelan woman named Claudia.

F: She's amazing.

D: Filling in all the blanks is really what people miss out on. They think they just work hard in the office all the time and that will do it. It's not about how much you do, it's about who you become in the process. If you don't change yourself and don't become something, you really won't make the big strides. You'll make some money, you'll get somewhere, but you won't get everything, and I want everything.

F: This has been an easy journey for you, right? The last five years must have been like candy canes and lollipops, it's just been super easy for you I would assume?

D: Oh, yeah, super easy. No, not at all. I mean, there were multiple experiences I can look back on and say, this sucks. I just don't want to deal with this anymore. The big pressure of accountability, the big pressure of external people when you're doing what you're doing like being on stage in a way, people are looking at you, waiting for you to either make it or fail, usually fail.

Especially my family. My brothers that I grew up with are all a couple of years older. My parents, although they want what's best for me, they still want me to be safe, and going out and doing what I'm doing is not the safe way. I could fail hard and, in their eyes, they'd rather me not try so I don't fail, which in my head just doesn't work for me.

It's been very hard. Lots of times I've wanted to stop and quit and get off the team and get away from accountability. Looking back, what I did was I leaned into the accountability.

F: The proof that this is all working out for you is, we're sitting right now in the backyard of your house, right?

D: Oh, yeah. It's a duplex, Downtown--

F: When I first met you, you didn't even have an apartment yet.

D: Yes, I remember that.

F: So many people that are in your generation that we've talked to don't believe the American Dream is possible. They feel that it's something that was a thing back in the day, as of this new millennium, it's not possible anymore. Based on what you've achieved, in the process that you've taken, what would you say to that?

D: I mean, the American dream, I guess, is perceived differently these days. It used to be buying a house, getting married, starting a family, and getting a dog. The kids that I know, their parents were pretty well off. They didn't have to go out and work that hard for this. My parents did okay, but raising five kids that can be financially obligating. So, I don't remember getting a lot of things handed to me early on. I was always told, you're raised to work hard. If you want those nice things, you've got to work for it. No one's gonna give it to you.

Then the second I got into real estate that was a big eye-opener because to make money in real estate, you have to go up against a lot of realtors and a lot of objections. Most people are not able to say yes to that because they think they can't do it. If you start learning early and often about failing and about handling objections, I think that's what a lot of the people in my generation didn't do

F: Do you believe that The American Dream is still possible?

D: Oh, yeah. I mean, I did it. If the American dream was buying your house, finding someone to marry, buying a dog, building a business, building enough for you and others around you, then I'm on my way to checking off all those boxes right this second.

F: Before you're 30?

D: Before I'm 30, yes, which is three years away.

F: If you talk to people who did very well pre-year 2000, before the tech boom, they would say, it's a lot more difficult now because of all the distractions to stay focused and drill down and do what needs to be done. How did you avoid the distractions? I've known you for a while and you've had some tragedy in your family. There's been a lot of stuff that's been able to distract you and derail you pretty quickly, and it didn't happen to you.

D: That's a great question. Distractions are hard. I will be the first one to say that I'm not nearly as efficient with my time as I should be. I think the way I've dealt with the distraction is, I just spent more time with my head down making the results. I spent more time with the right people, and I just spent more time doing it than others were willing to. I stay focused on my tasks, habits, and rituals. That is how we win.

F: I think what's even more remarkable is that there's a distraction that you have in your life that you brought onto yourself, becoming an Iron Man. The training on what it takes to be a triathlete and to compete in multiple Ironman competitions. It's an actual career for you at this point, you're an athlete at the highest level.

That is a distraction in itself. I know when I was working side by side with you. By the time you made your first phone call, you'd been up for three or four hours already just doing swims and running. Then when we finished our workday, there was David downtown jogging around Lake Eola until the sun goes down and he can't see anymore. Despite that distraction, you still accomplished results in business and your personal life. Talk to me about the Ironman journey.

D: The Ironman journey started when Dan Grieb told me to go get in shape. I was a whopping 220 pounds. I was not in good shape, I could barely run a mile. I couldn't run around the corner.

F: Where are you now?

D: Now I'm hovering around 171-175 lbs. I'm a little heavier than I want to be, but I'm getting back to it. The lowest that I got to was 149lbs. It was very early when I joined the team. April 2015, when I went to my first gym session, and then six months, down the road, we got into half marathons and running. I signed up for the Disney marathon in January of 2016 and that was going to be my first marathon.

Training for that around September, I was in the best shape of my life. I was training with Dan, and I was running with a track shack here in downtown Orlando. I don't know, the idea just came to me where I said, *"You know what? Fit people do triathlons. I'm a fit person."* In my head, I told myself, *"I'm as fit as I've ever been. So why don't I just do a triathlon?"*

I signed up for a sprint with my older brother. I was training for a couple of weeks going into the swimming pool doing 800 yards swims, a 12-mile bike ride, and then a 3.1-mile run. About a week before the race my older brother said, *"Hey, I'm not gonna make it to the race."* I thought, what am I gonna do? I went to Dan and told him I have this extra registration for this sprint in one week and did he want to join? Dan said, *"Hell yeah."* We did the race together. That's how it started, you get addicted after your first one.

We signed up for another sprint. Then quickly after that, Dan found a coach, Hector Torres in Orlando for the Ironman. He had a tri club in Orlando, we started training with them. That's how I found out about the Ironman. I didn't know the full Ironman is a 2.4-mile swim followed by a 112-mile bike ride, and then you run a 26.2-mile run a full marathon.

F: Voluntarily.

D: Voluntarily, all in one day, starting at 7 am. You have until midnight that same day to complete it. So, people are taking 17 hours or more to finish these races. When I heard about that I thought, *"That's crazy. Never doing that."* Dan said, *"Hey, there's a race coming up in Panama City Beach, let's go volunteer."* So, we drove to Panama City Beach and volunteered at the race.

We both were inspired by what we saw. All shapes, all sizes, all ages, youngest was 18 years old, oldest was 70 plus, running this full Ironman. I thought, *"There's no reason we can't do this."* We signed up for that race one year later. If you volunteer, you get immediate registration for next year. We signed up the day after that race.

That gave us one whole year to start training. We did a bunch of races that year, non-Ironman, like 5K's and 10K's and marathons and triathlons. November 2017, we completed our first Ironman together. Since then, between Dan and I, we are going on 30 plus completed Ironman races. That's including half and full's between him and I. Me personally, I did my fourth full last year and I have done nine half Ironmen.

F: This also brought your family closer together, right? Your brother has been doing some?

D: Yes, shortly after, I don't remember exactly how it all worked out, Robbie, my younger brother, was always in decent shape. I just dragged Robbie in, he came and did a couple of sprints with me. Then he caught the bug pretty quick. He got into running, biking and training. He has completed one full Ironman, three half Ironmen., and we both qualified for the World Championship in the 17.3 Ironman, which took us to South Africa.

F: Where does that rank on your level of personal accomplishments?

D: It's high. Neither he nor I had ever traveled to South Africa. We spent 14 days going from here to New York to Johannesburg, and Port Elizabeth competed and then went on a couple of safaris. South Africa is beautiful, absolutely beautiful.

F: You said that's up there in your accomplishments, What is number 1?

D: I would go back to completing my first Ironman. Up until that point, for my whole life, I'd been out of shape. I didn't feel very attractive and I didn't feel very in shape mentally or physically. To complete the first full Ironman, going from where I was, brought me to tears.

There's a video of me crossing the finish line, and I'm just bawling. It brought me to such emotional depths. A depth that I'd never been to. I went from being 220 pounds just about two years before, to finishing a full Ironman in a formidable time. It was 13 hours and four minutes, which is good for me. That was a big deal.

F: In conclusion here, what's next for David? You are in your 20s, you've done more before the age of twenty-seven than a lot of people do in a lifetime. The whole purpose of what we're doing here with this book *"The Process,"* is having somebody like you come here and interview for the book to talk about how we can duplicate this across the world. So, the world itself can feel like this is all possible. Now you're 27, you've done a lot. What's next?

D: What's next? Well, I'm leaning into the wealth side of things. I'm focusing on putting away as much money as I can, investing in the right places. Investing in myself so that I can make this year, and every year until I retire, my best year ever. Working less and making more, and spending more time with my soon-to-be wife.

What's next is just building the future. Don't worry about where I am today, just worry about where I want to be 10 years from now. Just act as if I am 10 years older. If I keep on the trajectory I am on now, I'll be set for life in a matter of 10 years, or maybe sooner.

F: That's awesome. We appreciate you for allowing us to take some of your processes, duplicate them, put them here in print, and let other people read them. If you have one last thing to say to anybody reading this book who has any limiting belief about accomplishing what you've done, or even more, what would you tell them?

D: I would say, limiting beliefs are so restricting. In my head, I'm very optimistic. If you ask most people who know me, the one thing they'll say is, *"David is the most optimistic person that I know."* If you feel like you can't do something or if you feel like that's not for you, you're never gonna get there. You just gotta get that out of your head as fast as you can. Surround yourself with people who are all wanting to push you and you push yourself.

Build something bigger, because like I said, I'm very optimistic no matter what the challenge. It could be, *"David, you're gonna go make a million dollars next year."* Great. I can do it. There is always a way, I'll find the way, I'll find the right people who are doing it, and I'll do exactly what they do, and I'll get there. People will joke, they'll say, *"David always says, it's okay, we'll figure it out, we'll find a way."* That's indeed exactly what I do. If you try hard enough, you'll find the way.

F: I appreciate the way you keep pouring into people. Congratulations on your engagement to your future beautiful wife, and let's catch up very soon.

D: Thank you so much. Thanks for having me.

TYLER TRAINER INTERVIEW

The Tyler Trainer story can be described simply as one of resourcefulness. Tyler took something he has an extreme passion for, and using nothing more than the resources at his disposal, created a service business that so many people are enjoying the results of. It is a perfect example of someone who believes in an idea and follows a series of processes to make it a reality. Tyler's journey has been a lot of fun to watch.

F: I am here with Tyler Trainer of Winter Garden Florida. Tyler, What's the name of your company?

T: Nxt Level cuisine.

F: Nxt Level cuisine. You've been in the restaurant business for a while now. How old are you?

T: I'm 23. I've been in a restaurant since I was 15.

F: 15 and as of right now, you're a chef at one of the most prestigious places in Central Florida, isn't that right?

T: Yes.

F: What got you interested in the food industry?

T: Well, I've always loved food. A running joke in my family is my Dad cooks on the grill, and my mom cooks in the microwave. Other than the special nights a week where my dad was able to cook on the grill, I was pretty much left to fend for myself. It started when I was eight years old, I made a key lime pie for my Dad's birthday.

F: Eight years old, doing key lime pie for your dad's birthday. How did it come out?

T: He said it was the best key lime pie he's ever had. So I haven't changed the recipe since.

F: That's one of your biggest selling products at "NXT level cuisine", right?

T: Yes.

F: You're eight years old, you made a pie, then what happened?

T: I continued just doing little baking jobs. One of my neighbors hired me to make a birthday cake for his wife's 50th birthday party. Just little jobs like that. When I got to high school I did dual enrollment. This means I spent three periods out of my day at one of the tech schools, and then go back for the rest of my classes. For three periods out of my day, I was doing culinary at one of the tech schools.

F: What made you say, you know what, I think I'm gonna take a crack at this and just start "Nxt Level Cuisine."

T: Nxt Level cuisine started, actually, during the 2020 pandemic quarantine. My two other friends and I were looking for something to do. I've always wanted to try to start it and just took a crack at it. We haven't looked back since.

F: That's great! Our families have been friends for half a decade now, and we've rarely ever gotten to hang out because you're always on the road doing something. Tell us about your weekly schedule to be able to maintain being a chef and running this business.

T: I'm working five or six days a week at the hotel, and when I'm not doing that, especially since the beginning of this year, I've been working on Nxt Level Cuisine.

F: So how many hours do you think you're putting in between both things?

T: I'm putting 50 to 60 hours in at the hotel, and then the rest of the time, at Nxt Level Cuisine. As soon as I got off of work, as soon as I got to my car, I was on the phone with my other two friends working on it. I was putting at least 20, 30 hours a week in preparation for the holidays.

F: Two full-time jobs?

T: Yes.

F: So why go through all that?

T: Well, the way I've always been raised is you gotta work for what you want. You put the time in. It may not always come out perfect every time, but you have got to keep trying.

F: Especially at the beginning of a business, one of the things you realize is, you can't always guarantee the result, but you owe yourself the effort.

T: Exactly.

F: Without effort what else is there? I mean, it's been over a couple of hundred years that we've been a country. People have come from all parts of the world to come to make a life here. If you listen to their story, it's the same thing. Get here, work hard, and have what you want. We may not live in the same period as they did in 1776, but the principles are still the same, aren't they?

T: Yes you just have to find a way to adapt to your current situation. Right now in the social media generation that we're in, we have such an advantage with Facebook and Instagram. Using these tools and adding an enormous amount of effort is what makes success happen.

F: Which can be a distraction. So how do you use those platforms as an empowering thing for your business and not a distraction? There are a lot of distractions that can come with all that.

T: The main thing we use it for is just to keep our client base up to date. It is a great way to keep clients informed.

F: What about you as an individual who's in a younger part of their life, there's a lot of distractions for you there too. Things like technology, the media, a lot is going on right now. What do you do to keep the distractions to a minimum so you can focus on your business?

T: I just stay focused. Honestly, one of my biggest things is if I stay focused on something, it usually turns out well. I've always had a hard time focusing my entire life, with tests, school, all that stuff. Never really was the greatest at it. The stuff that I'm passionate about, I can stay focused on.

F: How many businesses have you owned before this one?

T: Officially, none. Back when I was younger, my parents during Christmas gave me business cards for a company called Pie in the Sky. It was just me selling pies and cakes to my neighbors and my parents' friends.

F: What kind of growth have you seen in your business month over month?

T: Our first big drop was in October 2020 for Halloween. Then on Thanksgiving, we blew up. We grew 500% in one month.

F: That's a big number.

T: Yes, it was just all getting our name out there. We got Orlando Weekly's Instagram to do a post on us. We were on all these different Reddit pages promoting and were just all in finding these different avenues to get our name out there. If we got people to look at the website, they'll order something.

F: Where are you now?

T: We have been growing about 50% every month.

F: What's the vision?

T: Farmers markets, then after that, I want to start going to people's houses and be a chef for hire. If somebody wants a romantic evening or something like that. The vision for me in the long term is that it will be my full-time career.

F: How many employees do you have?

T: Right now we have three people, one doing the social media site, one doing the finances, and then me in the kitchen. Soon I'm gonna need some more hands in the kitchen.

F: Do you think you'll be at that point of being able to walk away from the day job at the hotel? In three years, five years? What's the number for you?

T: I would say three years at the earliest, five years at the max as long as I can keep it going, and keep people interested in it.

F: How old will you be then?

T: I'll be 26 or 28.

F: 26, so not even 30 yet. You'll be running your own business, doing your thing, doing what you love.

T: Exactly. Doing what I love never feels like work to me. That's the main reason why I started cooking. It just never felt like work to me.

F: Amazing story and journey. There are a lot of folks who don't start businesses out of fear. They all have great ideas and great vision, but they take no action. What would you say to somebody ready to make a move, but they are frozen solid on the business part of it?

T: Do research in the field that you want to get into. I feel like there's this misconception that you need all this financial backing when you're going to start a business. We started it when all three of us were out of jobs, we didn't have the financial backing. We didn't ask our parents for money. We didn't ask friends for money. We took the little bit of money that we had and made a website, got the domain, and we just started it. You don't need this crazy financial backing. You just got to apply yourself to it and figure out a way around it until you get that financial backing, and then you start climbing up the ladder with it.

F: What's the five-year vision for you personally?

T: In the long run, I want this to be all I do. Have employees cooking, delivering, running the whole show. That way we can serve as many people as we can.

F: How do you feel this fits into the vision of the American dream?

T: Well, I feel like the American Dream has always been just working hard to accomplish your dreams. I feel like a lot of people nowadays, especially my generation, once they fail once, they're done. They just say *"Oh well that's never gonna work I'm done. I'm just going to wash my hands of it."* Instead of just picking yourself back up and going at it again or trying it a different way.

There are a lot of people trying to start their businesses, and honestly, the market is more crowded than ever. Pretty much any market that you go into unless you're creating something new, you just have to find a way to get yourself stable and then climb your way up.

F: You're saying it hasn't always been easy?

T: I don't think it's ever been easy. People get discouraged so quickly. They just need to be able to teach themselves to pick themselves back up and keep going.

F: In your line of business right now, what are you looking at for rejection? Do you ever get some rejection, or reach out to people that are just not interested?

T: Oh, yeah. When I was applying to the Culinary Institute of America in New York for college, when I applied to my intern positions anywhere around the country, I think I applied to 15 places and I got three yeses. There's always gonna be rejection, it's never going to be a guaranteed thing.

F: You have had ups and downs even personally. Tell us about this car story, because for some people this would have stopped them in their tracks right there, and they would have quit.

T: I had just bought a car at the same time that we dropped our first drop for Nxt Level Cuisine. I think I bought the car on October 25th. Our first drop was on October 31st.

F: Did you finance it or pay cash?

T: Hundred percent cash. I saved up the money and bought it all cash and paid outright. It was mine, it was the first car that I had in my name. The first time I'm paying insurance, the full weight of my insurance is on my own. It was 100% mine. I got that in October and then it was late November a month afterward, I was on my way to work and I was stopped at a red light and then got rear-ended.

F: The person didn't have insurance, right?

T: No insurance, still dealing with the neck and back injury right now.

F: Just a wild thing to happen right in the middle of launching. It's funny, because there's a ceiling of achievement that we all have, and everybody has one. Everybody's natural ability will get them to their ceiling of achievement. Then it takes a little bit of grit and research, like you say, to break through that. Then, once you break through it, you get another ceiling of achievement. Then you're going to find a way to break through that.

We see so many times in coaching, people get to this first level of achievement, and they think about how hard it's going to be to break through it. Instead of putting the effort in, they say, *"Well, I'm gonna go start something else, because I think it'll be the path of least resistance."* Then it takes them two years to get back to another natural ceiling of achievement. Where if they just stayed the course, and spent the next few months breaking through their original ceiling. they'd be so much further along.

T: It's all about just navigating your way through it. Fail once, try again, fail again, try again. There's no reason to ever stop trying. Just find a different way to do it the next time. There's no staying comfortable. You always have to be on your toes and be prepared for anything. We always have to stay on our toes.

F: What's the next big push for your business?

T: Next big push? Right now, we're focusing on trying to get into Farmers Markets. That's our next big thing.

F: What's that process look like?

T: Depends on which one we go to. Right now, we're looking at a couple of ones here in the Central Florida area. A lot of them are full, we've gotten rejection emails from some. Raising capital for the equipment, hand washing stations, displays, we're all just planning it out right now. Then, in the middle of all that, get people to say yes.

F: I think that's what's so impressive about this story is that when the pandemic started, so many people retreated and got into scarcity mode, anything that they had that was ambitious, they just put it on the wayside and said, *"This is not the world for that."* You decided to take an opportunity where people were home and said, *"How do I get people what they want for the holidays and whatever else they want for during the week, and get it to them so they can have one less thing to think about."*

T: I've never been a person that can sit around and do nothing. I was going to be doing something.

F: Nxt Level Cuisine is the business. You're available on Facebook and Instagram?

T: Yes.

F: Cool. Thanks for hanging out with us. Tyler, we appreciate it. I think we learn a lot from these processes, so we appreciate the time.

T: I appreciate it.

ACKNOWLEDEGMENTS

I cannot express enough thanks to my editing team for their continued support and encouragement: Karla Hawley, MJ Coleman, Cidalia Zipeto, and Terry Gurno. I offer my sincere appreciation for the learning opportunities provided by you all. I could not have done this without you.

My completion of this book could not have been accomplished without the support of my family and business partners, both current partners and those from the past. Thank you for allowing me to be a part of your journey, as well as you being part of mine.

Thanks to my parents, Mr. and Mrs. Pasquale Zipeto. Their countless hours of life lessons and leadership made this book possible and me who I am today.

My daughter Lorelei, is my greatest accomplishment. The woman you are becoming inspires me daily. So very proud of you.

Finally, to my caring, loving, and supportive wife, Cidalia. My deepest gratitude. Your encouragement when times get rough is what drives me to continue to be better. My heartfelt thanks. I love you to the moon and back!

ABOUT THE AUTHOR

Francis Zipeto has professionally been in business for himself since 2009. He excelled in launching a career as a real estate salesperson in Massachusetts. In 2013, Francis chased his dream and moved to Orlando Florida, where he became the CEO of a Keller Williams Realty franchise office. Through his time as the Ceo, coaching, and training, became a passion of his.

In 2013, he attended his first Tony Robbins seminar in West Palm Beach, Florida. He witnessed firsthand how the art of coaching could impact so many lives. At that moment he decided to strive for a career in coaching and training. Francis is now an Executive Head Coach at Business Maps, one of the most prestigious coaching companies in North America.

He also has business partnerships and interests in real estate investing as the Quality Properties USA Partner Network co-founder. This company assists other real estate investors to get started in business using its proven systems and models.

Personally, he is the husband to his wife Cidalia, and a proud father to his daughter Lorelei. Together, they live in Orlando, Florida, and love to travel in their RV, play golf, and have competitive family game nights. Francis believes his greatest success is the designed life he has built with his wife and daughter.

CPSIA information can be obtained
at www.ICGtesting.com
Printed in the USA
LVHW080223050222
710279LV00007B/235